LOST
LEGENDS

30 YEARS 30 VOICES

LOST LEGENDS

30 YEARS 30 VOICES

Published by Serendipity

Serendipity
CL00.14, Clephan Building
De Montfort University
The Gateway, Leicester
LE1 9BH

+44 (0) 116 257 7316
info@serendipity-uk.com
www.serendipity-uk.com

Serendipity Artists Movement Limited
Company registration number in England and Wales
07248813
Charity registration number in England and Wales
1160035

Copyright © Serendipity Artists Movement Limited 2017

Cover Image © The Unloved

Design © theunloved.co.uk

Text © Joseph Allen, Mellow Baku, Pawlet Brookes, Pamela Campbell-Morris, Paulo Carnoth, George Cole, Derrick Evans, Dorothy Francis, Tony Graves, Cheddi Gore, Philip Herbert, Donna Jackman, Louise Katerega, Duncan Lawrence, Carol Leeming, Michael Lewis, Iris Lightfoote, Tara Lopez, Madu Messenger, Elvy Morton, Florence Chanakira-Nyahwa, Suzanne Overton-Edwards, Shakha Palmer, Victor Richards, Brian Simmonds, Gregory Smith, Julie D. Smith, Dianne Van-der-Westhuizen, Boston Williams, Quincy, Freedom Tariq Zampaladus.

Photographers © AFP, Aglana, Matt Cawrey, Don Cravens, David Fenton, Disney Enterprises, Suleman Garcia, Getty Images, Highfields Rangers, Sally Hossack, Hulton Archive, Kainé Management, Keystone, Leicester Mercury, Leicester Museums and Galleries, The LIFE Images Collection, SAUL LOEB, Mama Quilla, Marilyn Nance, Maull and Company, MPI, Ming de Nasty, Michael Ochs Archives, Laurie Rampling, Earle Robinson, Jurgen Schadeberg, Mike Sewell, Tom Simpson, Leni Sinclair, Elaine Smith, Smithsonian Institution, Theatre Royal Stratford East.

Editor © Pawlet Brookes

Project Researcher © Gemma Clarke

Additional Research © Amy Grain, Reneé Van-der-Westhuizen

ISBN: 978-0-9926319-4-9

Special thanks from Serendipity to: Paul Brookes and all contributors to Lost Legends

CONTENTS

INTRODUCTION

PAWLET BROOKES

Welcome to Lost Legends: 30 Years 30 Voices, a publication celebrating the last 30 years of Black History Month in the UK. The publication asks one question: *what does Black History Month mean to you?* This one question then opened up a series of unanswered questions, concerns and vision for history that was inclusive rather than subjective and one-sided.

The voices involved in 30 Years 30 Voices are all people who have a relationship with Leicester and have contributed to its development and to Black History Month through a number of different avenues such as arts, culture, sports and education. The voices tell a story of the African and African Caribbean community pushing to be recognised for their contribution and place in the making and shaping of history and ensuring that this information is passed on and recorded as legacy of their heritage.

All the voices raise questions and make statements about the emotional health and well-being of the African and African Caribbean community and how raising awareness would empower a community to have been recognised as contributing more to society than being purely part of the empire and new commonwealth but having a heritage and history that surpass what the average person is taught or is made of aware of through education.

So Black History Month was felt to be necessary and not just confined to October but was taking place 365 days a year. There was acknowledgement of the need for a celebratory month to keep it on the agenda and to act as a catalyst or aide memoire to the educational system and to historians that gaps in historical landscape largely could be filled by rewriting and filling in the gaps selectively excluded.

The stories and voices take you from Africa to the Caribbean and back to the UK showing the transatlantic triangle and the shaping of a global epidemic – amnesia with forgotten and hidden histories. Yet, the contributions have supported the development of the western world.

30 Years 30 Voices also includes a set of key milestones over the last 250 years largely from a British perspective; however, it is hard to not include some of the major achievements made by other great Africans and African Caribbeans across the diaspora. The milestones are split into two columns, one focused on an international and national picture and the other column more local. The rationale for this is to clearly outline how we are all part of history in its making and the pinch points that collide with international politics so that it is clear Black history is part of world history.

> *"Collecting and structuring the fragmented evidence of the Black past in Britain as well as in the Caribbean and Africa is a monumental task, but it is a major agenda item in [the] last decade of the twentieth century [to create a] better basis for achieving a fully multicultural British society"*
>
> Len Garrison (2006)

Finally, the hope is that this publication will be used to stimulate discussion, raise awareness and offer another perspective on history, recognising hidden histories and the Lost Legends.

Pawlet Brookes

6

Pawlet Brookes. Photographer The Unloved

LOST LEGENDS 30 YEARS 30 VOICES

ACTIV-ISTS

8

Highfields Rangers (1986-1987). Back row from left; T.Wager, R. Francis (manager), A Mensak, S. Paul, C. Buchanan, P. Rawle, M. Rowe, G. Rowe, I. Walker, M. Piper (coach), D. King (assistant manager). Front row from left; D. Rawle, D. Daley, N. Burke, J. Buchanan, R. Gerrard (mascot), D. Wright, P. Currie, P. Williams, J. Johnson.
Photograph reproduced with kind permission of Highfields Rangers

JOSEPH ALLEN

BLACK HISTORY MONTH 30 YEARS ON

I have been reflecting on the 30 years since the start of what is called Black History Month in Leicester, and indeed elsewhere in England. At its inception I wondered why this project came into being, what was its purpose and what difference was envisaged by its creators. Today I am still wondering.

On reflection Black History Month came into being as an appeasement strategy by the government of the time to quell dissension by the Black community. There was a fear that the alienation of the Black community from mainstream Britain could bring social unrest to inner city areas across the land.

Back in 1987 a group of people came together to lead Black History Month Leicester.

Members of the group included the Leicester Carnival, Raddle Books, Ajani, LUCA, Youth Foundation, Highfield Rangers, Spectrum and the Highfield Workshop Centre as the venue for the first event.

From memory the event was largely an artistic outflow from performing artists in the community. It was more of a fete with bits of information about Black heroes, such as Marcus Garvey, Martin Luther King JR, Malcolm X. There were also maps to Africa, the Caribbean and the World.

The group was essentially a collection of individuals who came together to promote the existence of Black people in Leicester. In the early years the same model of artistic outflow continued to be the main production of Leicester Black History Month, always at the Highfield Workshop or Spectrum.

Since the demise of these venues during the mid-1990s, the Black History Month became an ad-hoc production void of focused leadership, strategy, management, organisation, ownership and accountability. Why?

Firstly, to this day I am not aware of what Black History Month is, was or should be about. By its very title one could speculate that it could be about a reflection of the contribution of Black people in world affairs over the centuries?

One would also surmise that the intention was to both educate and celebrate that contribution particularly from an African and Caribbean perspective? And perhaps to add the American dimension?

From my observations, it is my contention that the purpose of Black History Month was never clarified. In that respect, it is not hard to forgive why there has been a lack of interest and participation from the wider Black community in Leicester and Leicestershire.

Secondly, if the question was asked who is responsible for planning, organising and delivering a programme for Black History Month, one would be utterly surprised if there was a satisfactory answer. In short, nobody is responsible, suffice to say that there are those who try to do something when the time comes.

Central to this situation is the lack of unity in Leicester's Black community.

Whether this is to do with an island mentality that persists in the city; whether it's to do with apathy that persists in the city; whether it is due to nepotism that persists in the city; whether it's due to personality differences that

9

persist in the city; or whether it's a lack of essential skills; the fact remains that, though often meaningful, good opportunities to improve the status of Black people are more often than not missed.

Thirdly, the lack of meaningful input from the public sector in the city contributes to the ad hoc nature of Black History Month in Leicester. In 2015 I attended perhaps one the best examples of Black History Month at the Leicester City Hall. It was an artistic demonstration of Black music by women over the last 60 years or so.

What I noted was the speech of the City Mayor. He bigged up the importance and contribution of Black people in the City. Though I believed what was expressed, I often wonder why Black History Month is not connected to the cultural programmes delivered by the City Council in real terms.

And what is the contribution of the City Council and the County Council for that matter?

To underline the last 30 years of Black History Month, it is my simple opinion that the whole initiative has been flawed from its inception to this day. The flaws are to do with the inability or reluctance of the Black community in Leicester to work together in a cohesive manner for the betterment of all of us in the City.

So what of the future for the Black history project?

To my mind the initiative should go back to basics. In future it should proceed on the basis of maximum feasible community participation in the focus of intent, including the content, the planning, the organising, the management and the delivery.

Further the participants should include young people who should be primary in learning and understanding the contribution of Black people in the life of Leicester, Britain, Caribbean, African and American and world evolution past, present and future.

The initiative should develop in a partnership strategy with the public, private and voluntary sector Leicester or Leicestershire to demonstrate our sense of belonging and contribution.

COUNCILLOR GEORGE COLE

DO WE STILL NEED BLACK HISTORY MONTH?

The question as to whether Black History Month should continue seemed an odd question to ask Black people living in the diaspora, under a European-led Government. When Dr Carter G. Woodson, the son of ex-slaves started the Association for the Study of Negro Life and History back in 1915, and later Negro History Week in 1926, the organisation and celebrations many see as the forerunner to Black History Month, he did it because Black people were largely not represented in history books written by European historians and when they were, invariably they were misrepresented. Therefore, the question that must be asked is has anything changed since then? One area to examine in the search for an answer is schools. It is important to examine this institution because many would argue that the primary function of the school system is to condition the minds of our venerable children and to put knowledge into their minds to support that conditioning. These children then become the next generation of leaders in society, who make decisions that impact on the lives of others living under their rule. Therefore, one effective way of reversing the problem identified by Dr Carter G. Woodson is to root the changes in education, with particular emphasis on the education children received in school from an early age.

As someone who went through the European education system, both in the Caribbean and in England in the sixties, I experienced the lack of representation and the misrepresentation, which served to deny me of my true identity, and to hide from me the vast contributions Black people have made to world civilisation, in so many different ways. I have children who went through the education system in the United Kingdom in the eighties, nineties and noughties and they told me, 'not a lot had changed from the sixties'. There are a few tokenisms but no real substantial changes have taken place, where children are enlightened about the true facts relating to Black people and the positive roles they have played in civilisation over the years.

Given that Black History Month started in 1976 in America as a direct development of Dr Carter G. Woodson and others' strenuous work and a decade later in the UK, it is reasonable to believe that significant changes could have taken place in schools during the period of my children's journey through school. Now I have grandchildren who will be starting school in the next few years, it would be a significant indictment against the government of the UK if it transpired that their experience of Black History in school is not much different from their parents and grandparents. Institutional racism in schools is nothing new. The government has the powers to change it. But when we see one of the recent secretaries of state for education wanted to remove Mary Seacole from the school curriculum it tells us that the government itself is a racist institution. If that be the case, then the need for Black History Month and its aims of celebrating Black History and bringing to the fore the true role and contribution of Black people in civilisation, is as great today as it was back in the days when Dr Carter G. Woodson first started on his journey to correct a serious wrong being perpetrated against Black people by white people, and with Brexit being in vogue at present the need has never been greater.

11

12

Carter G Woodson, *Scurlock Studio Records,* Reproduced with permission of the Archives Center, National Museum of American History, Smithsonian Institution.

It is possible to argue that much has changed, in the representation and the presentation of Black people, in popular culture and other institutions, over the thirty years of Black History Month, and going back further to when Dr Carter G. Woodson started. We see it in the music industry, which spills over into the fashion industry, the everyday language, in the theatre, films and food to name but a few. Tenuous changes can be seen in the school system, in the form of Black teachers, lecturers and governors, in businesses and in politics. Many would argue that Barack Obama's election to one of the most powerful leadership positions in the world was as a direct result of Black History Month bringing Black people, more and more, to the consciousness of the masses. We see changes that have taken place in the legal systems, in the more readily acceptance by the wider society of interracial friendship and matters of the heart. The dense racial and cultural mix in society could also be attributed to the contributions of Black History Month. However, many would argue that all these apparent achievements are superficial and can be blown over, blown off course, by the slightest change in the racial breeze in the country, as can be seen by the effect of Brexit in the UK and the election of Donald Trump in the USA.

The banks still have racial problems lending money to Black people; employers are still being taken to the courts over racial bias in their employment practices; boardrooms of businesses still have problems letting in Black faces; and the default position of the vast majority of white people in society as a whole is to see Black people in a negative light, as scientific evidence has

13

shown through experiments. It is important to note that those experiments also show that Black people have that default position.

If the question was asked which race of people invented the fastest computer in the world and received the equivalent of a Nobel Prize for it, who invented Micro-Fresh a product invented to eliminate harmful bacteria from the home and environment, who invented blood transfusion, the water gun or home security system, I doubt many, or if anyone, would say the Black race. Yet they were invented by Black people, and the vast majority of these inventions are very recent. How many of us know that Beethoven had Black blood in him? Yet, if his notoriety for music was instead for criminality we would all know him as a Black person.

Black History Month has a job to do, a job that is nowhere near completion. Its journey to achieve the objective it set itself is a perpetual one. It is a job that only Black people can be relied upon to do in good conscience; and we must be wary of others calling themselves Black thereby hijacking the work started by Dr Carter G. Woodson for their own end, as is currently taking place. When Dr Carter G. Woodson set off on his journey, to right a wrong, it was clear in his mind who was written out of history for the most part and misrepresented by historians' pens.

66 Black History Month was needed in Britain because the black past had been largely buried and it was during the 1980s that the task of exhumation took on real urgency. Unusually, history became critical to a whole community, while at the same time becoming highly personal to those who discovered it. 99

David Olusoga (2016)

CHEDDI GORE

SPORT AND ITS PLACE WITHIN BLACK HISTORY MONTH

I've always loved sport as far back as I can remember. I went to do a Sports Leadership Qualification at college and even when I went into the forces, I was a keen sports person. I completed parachute training and was sent to Germany with a sporting regiment because I was half decent at football and boxing, and went on to Kenya, Cyprus and all around Europe. When I returned to Leicester in 1987, I wanted to work in sports and luckily enough I got a job at Granby Hall's Leisure Centre, which was run by Leicester City Council. It wasn't until I joined Leicester City Council's Black Workers Group, and then heard some of the issues which Black people are facing on a day to day basis that I recognised the importance of Black History Month. I went along to these meetings and listened and learnt a lot from my colleagues. I was then nominated to be the vice-chair of the group and really got my teeth into working on the equality agenda.

Later on, I applied for a job promoting racial equality in sport with Sport England and the Leicester Racial Equality Council, promoting Race Equality in Sport, as at that time there was a lot more information around issues facing ethnic minority communities when it comes to sport participation. It doesn't matter what sector we're working in there isn't a level playing field and because sport is my passion I wanted to see how I could affect change within the sports sector. Which leads me to my current role within an organisation called Sported, an East Midlands based capacity-building organisation designed really to support organisations that use sport to develop young people. The organisation was set up by Keith Mills, who was deputy chairman of the London Organising Committee of the Olympic and Paralympic Games (LOCOG) in 2012. He set up Sported as he felt that there was a lot of people who were disadvantaged and deprived and who weren't accessing sports provision to make sure we met their aims, and it has been fantastic how it has developed over the years.

In terms of how things have changed over the years, there are pockets of good practice but for a generation of Black people it's not enough. You often talk about this glass ceiling, sometimes you can actually see it in operation. We often play a good game in terms of Race Equality in sport, say the right things, we sometimes do the right things but there's a lack of commitment in terms of making real change and you know when real change happens because it's happened. But most of the time it's just talking about it "we will do this, we will do that" but nothing seems to ever get done. In that sense so we have to be mindful of that and when we get people who are really saying look "x needs to be done y needs to be done" it's not moaning, it's about wanting that level playing field for young people to make sure that they can access the same provisions as everyone else, and not just sport, as health and well-being are also important for everyone.

When I went to my first Sport and Development Conference back in 1989 out of about 400 people there were only about three Black people there. I could not believe it; I always remember how I felt and the realisation that we were not included, so, yes I just could not believe it. I thought hold on a minute there's got to be more Black people than this who work in sport. I just cannot understand for the life of me why there's not more Black people in the sports sector. They might be thinking the same as some of the other footballers over in the 70s and 80s; 'there's no place for me there, I'm not going to get recognised for what I do so I'm going to go do something else'. I would like to see more young Black people in the world of sport whether that's participating, in the administration of sport, or management of sport.

Growing up in the 70s there was nothing about Black History Month. If you looked at the television, remember we only had about three channels, and it was very unlikely that you would see anybody resembling you. We yearned for Black history to be taught because people would then see something different than the negativity and stereotypical representations of Black people. So when Black History Month became a thing, I thought it was a great learning curve for people like me to really delve into Black history. I think as we get older we need more Black history spread throughout the year. I think then people would look at Black people in a different light, a positive light. Especially with the forces, thousands of Black people gave their lives for the Mother Country throughout the First and Second World Wars. There's no normal reason why that shouldn't be taught about in schools. If young people understand and recognise that it's all people, all communities that fought in the First and Second World Wars it's getting at a basic human condition whereby if you know somewhere that has supported you and helped you it's no good throwing stones at them. But that resonates with me, I think, because I've been in the forces. Surely a civilised country like Britain should recognise a thing like that.

So my honest opinion is that Black History Month needs to stay but the issues it highlights shouldn't be confined to just October. I'd like to see things happening in January, when people are down and people are depressed about Christmas, we could have something about Black history, the arts, sport. I mean if you look at sports and Black history, it's huge and no one is looking at the points. Where have all our Black players gone from 1970 – 1980? You don't see them because of the glass ceiling. They know that they won't get the opportunities but there's no rationale or reason why those guys who are skilled, have got the ability and talent, that can go into coaching and managing, but yet you don't see those faces. So across sport, across all sectors, you want those pioneers, you want those leaders to say 'hold on a minute, this can't continue'. It's a struggle for individuals and collectives to make sure that the impact, the positive impact towards Black people in regards to whatever sector they are working in or operating. We as Black people are not moaners; we just want to make sure that it's a level playing field.

It's thirty years and you can see the process of what is happening, and you imagine in thirty years' time if someone is reading this they might be thinking, 'I'm glad we're not living back in 2017'. I'm hoping that they would say that they wouldn't want to live in 2017. It is really important to capture some of these things because I'm sure that it would in the test of time be some kind of positive for someone to say 'well look this is how they live then', he is not a reporter, this is a person working in the city, he's got no axes to grind but he wanted to make sure you get a good representation of how things have been.

16

Cyrille Regis, *playing for West Bromwich Albion (1980).* Photographer Laurie Rampling

TONY GRAVES

BLACK HISTORY MONTH – REPRESENTATION OR RECOGNITION?

Many of the memories I have of Black History Month are as a result of the work I have delivered over the years as an arts programmer and producer. It has provided me with some of the best moments and experiences but also considerable challenges and frustration. At the centre is the struggle between representation and recognition. Let me explain what I mean. Many theatres, arts centres, museums, galleries and venues up and down the country try to ensure that there is a programme of work in Black History Month that celebrates cultural diversity and attracts a Black Asian Minority Ethnic (BAME) audience as well as non-BAME audiences.

This has been a catalyst for some great initiatives down the years. A project I produced in 1999 with a number of artists in Leicester called Vision Re: Afrika comes to mind. Commissioned by Leicester's New Walk Museum as a major part of its Black History Month programme for that year, it centred on mounting an exhibition of the museum's collections from across Africa, ranging from Egypt to Ethiopia. It enabled visitors to see exhibits that had previously been locked away in the vaults. In particular it corrected the previous misinterpretation of some of those pieces, as the exhibition was curated by the late modern day griot and historian, the wonderful Wolde Selassie. A number of exciting contemporary dance pieces were commissioned alongside, including one by the choreographer Sheron Wray, performed by Louise Katerega within the museum's main gallery and exhibition space. To me this project embodied the essence of Black History Month in terms of combining important education about our achievements and history as well as shining a light on the quality of our artistic expression.

Looking back however I have to admit that as much as I have good memories of this and other similar projects, I also recall Black History Month (especially the months leading up to it) as being a time of stress, mainly due to the expectations and pressure in being responsible for a particular venue's offering for the month. This was magnified by the fact that responsibility for its delivery often lay entirely at my door, something others who were similarly charged with producing a programme for Black History Month might have felt.

This did nothing to ease the underlying feeling that Black History Month provides a prescriptive and convenient format for many arts organisations to carry out their duty in respect of BAME artists and audiences before going back to business as usual. My response to this, and that of others I suspect, was to see it as an opportunity to create work that otherwise would not have been possible to produce. An example is the play 'Streets Paved with Gold' by Victor Richards which over a period of twenty years or so has gone on to achieve many triumphs since it emerged as a project within Black History Month some two decades ago.

It is understandable perhaps, for some of the reasons above, that I have a certain amount of ambivalence about the way in which Black History Month is approached and perhaps more importantly what it unintentionally perpetuates. My ambivalence can best be summed up by two connected but also differing ideas - 'representation' and 'recognition'. Both of these concepts are explored in the writing of Canadian philosopher Charles Taylor in his paper 'The Politics of Recognition' in which he examines thinking around our approach to notions of cultural

Wolde Selassie. Photographer Earle Robinson.

19

difference. It highlights the fact that representation, (as in the case of Black History Month - literally showing or representing people and their arts within programmes so that they are visible), although a laudable aim should not be an end in itself.

There is no doubting the importance of making visible via a dedicated season, (promoted in brochures, websites and social media), the work of Black artists for audiences, BAME or otherwise. Black History Month, in the terms I have previously outlined, achieves that. But if we content ourselves purely with increasing visibility then we are only addressing one element of a bigger picture in relation to the issues of access to resources and funding in order to create that work in the first place. Representation, though important, is only half the story.

I would argue that gaining recognition is of greater concern and has a much deeper, political resonance. Recognition is not representation for a limited period and then back to business as usual. Recognition addresses issues of power and relates to the value a system that governs who has access to decision-making, distribution of resources and funding. It means recognising the value inherent in culturally diverse art and arts practices so that they are seen not as interesting diversions from the 'norm', celebrated during Black History Month, but of equal value and importance and therefore of relevance to Black and white audiences all year round.

So looking back at my involvement from the perspective of a producer and programmer, at the same time as celebrating its anniversary, it is important to ensure that Black History Month does not play into the narrative concerned purely with representation. It is part of a wider acknowledgement that we have to change the value systems within society so that the status quo is shifted. This will help establish the ethos and goals behind Black History Month throughout our various institutions, arts based or otherwise, and within the fabric of our society. In this way we can achieve both representation and recognition for our historical and continuing contribution to not just arts and culture but all the other aspects of human achievement in which Black people have been integral throughout history.

SUZANNE OVERTON-EDWARDS

YES WE CAN

Black History Month is a period that I look forward to. It is a time when I will learn more about the contributions that Black people have made to society in so many ways across the years and to current times. It is a time of heightened awareness of the pride that I feel as a Black woman and an unusually constructive and welcomed focus on Black people. It is one of the times when I reflect on the current state of affairs in Britain and across the world and consider, again, how Black people are perceived by society. So, Black History Month means a lot to me.

As an educationalist, I have witnessed the positive impact that the month's activities have on individual students, the way in which it has added a different type of glue to students' friendships, encouraged their deeper thinking about who they are and what their predecessors have achieved. It gives them inspiration, challenges the assumptions that they make about themselves and others and encourages them to be more aspirational. It has made them ask questions, learn about issues, value previous struggles and put them into a context of current issues that blight the world. Amongst some students, I see the stimulus to work harder, to become more focused to achieve their goal. They adopt the attitude of *"others have done it before us therefore why can't we, why can't you?"* As Barack Obama said, *"Yes we can"*. I have also seen the positive impact on students who are not Black. They have had the opportunity to learn, to appreciate different perspectives on life, to view their colleague students differently with a new understanding of the contributions that their ancestors have made and to have a small insight into what has gone into the make-up of their friends, colleagues and neighbours.

Their thinking is challenged and stretched; something that we all benefit from. In current times of "fake news", Brexit, Trump being President of the USA and the rise of the political right in Europe, there is a lot to learn from our histories. So, Black History Month means a lot to my students and me.

My daughter went to a school, where the pupils and staff were predominately white. She and her Black and mixed race friends were offended at the response they received when they asked staff about not celebrating Black History Month. The girls were articulate, had the backing of their parents and felt the need to change the culture of the school, for the benefit of all pupils and staff. The feeling seemed to be one of *we don't have a problem here, therefore there is nothing to fix and therefore there is no need to celebrate or even have a nodding acknowledgement to the need for Black History Month*. The girls organised an assembly with minimal support. The school did not understand that young people live in a mixed society and that they need to understand other people and develop tolerance and respect for differences. There seemed to be no recognition that diversity enriches the lives of everyone. Young people, in particular, should be hungry to learn about other people. That, to my way of thinking, is also what education is about, not simply gaining qualifications. It is also about preparing young people to become effective citizens of the world.

US President Barack Obama waves after addressing the NAACP Hundredth Anniversary convention in New York. *(16 July 2009).* Photograph reproduced with permission of SAUL LOEB/AFP/Getty Images.

My son's view of his experience of Black History Month at school was that it was mentioned in assembly, with a fleeting reference to it during history lessons, but always in the context of slavery. "I think that there is a little more to our history than just slavery" he said.

There are so many potential benefits for young people who have a high level of interest in others. It makes them more accepting, it encourages them to question the status quo and to really think for themselves, to challenge their own assumptions and continue with this process throughout their lives. With a minimal effort, every educational establishment at primary, secondary and tertiary level in urban and rural areas can acknowledge Black History Month in a constructive manner. If students become more aware at a young age there is a greater hope that they will see the benefits of having an inclusive approach to life. So, Black History Month means a lot to young people everywhere, my family and me.

I look forward to the day when there is no longer a need for Black History Month because our histories will be fully integrated into the curriculum and society. I look forward to the day when analyses are not purely Eurocentric but are fully inclusive. I look forward to the day when there is balanced reporting and scrutiny of past and current events. Sadly, I doubt that the time will be within my lifespan. To try practising what I preach, it is fair to say that things have improved during my life. That is a reflection of a changing, more accepting society. It also denotes changes in what becomes acceptable, for example, language that is used. However, it does not necessarily indicate that everyone's views have changed to become more tolerant and appreciative of those who are different

23

to themselves. In some people the "isms" have gone underground and people will think in a certain way but they will not overtly reveal their stance, although their true feelings will be manifested in some way that at best will cause discomfort and at worst real pain.

So there continues to be a need for Black History Month for society for my family and for me. We still have a long way to go, we are making progress but it is slow. We need to continue working together to get the embedded improvements and hopefully at some point in the not too distant future, there will no longer be a need for Black History Month.

"I think you always need the double perspective. Before you say that you have to understand what it is like to come from that "other" place. How it feels to live in that closed world. How such ideas have kept people together in the face of all that has happened to them. But you also have to be true to your own culture of debate and you have to find some way to begin to translate between those two cultures. It is not easy, but it is necessary.**"**

Stuart Hall (Adams and Hall, 2007)

MICHAEL LEWIS

THE LONGEST JOB TITLE

I see Black History Month as a celebration of life. It is the celebration of the history that was not given to me at junior or secondary school until I reached my late teens and asked more in-depth questions about the history and culture we were taught at school.

Black History Month is also one of the many battles I had to fight for professionally for the first eight years of my career, as Leicestershire's only Black librarian. Essentially it was my battlefield when it originally started to be acknowledged in Leicester. I had to prove to my associates in the so-called conscious community, that I was worthy of being involved. In an era of people being defined by what they wore and the music they listened to, I was out of place. I wasn't your typical reggae listening Black man and had taken a lot of negative comments from people I had grown up with in the community because not only was I a librarian, but more importantly I was seen as not being radical enough.

I was also fighting another battle with the traditional experienced professional librarians who would say openly (but not when I was within earshot) that Black people didn't read and questioned why my post - Assistant Librarian, Ethnic Minorities, African Caribbean Communities, the longest job title I have ever had - was ever established. I was also not a typical librarian. I argued my point, fought my corner and developed book collections that to their surprise were successful in their libraries and I wouldn't kowtow to managers. I took it upon myself to convince the library service to embrace the concept of Black History Month and use it as a platform to educate our communities, and bring the African Caribbean collections to life.

As a schoolchild I found myself asking lots of questions but didn't get the answers I sought from my local library. How did Captain Cook discover a continent already populated by Black people? How did Christopher Columbus discover a place populated by Native Americans? Teachers did not or could not answer my questions because this meant steering us away from a system that they had learnt at university and wanted us to embrace on a national level. My local library in the heart of Highfields, one of the most prominent multi-cultural communities in the heart of Leicester, could only reinforce the stereotypical histories we had been given at school. However, it also gave me Encyclopaedia Britannica, the Google or Wikipedia of the day, which became my tool to gain insights into discovering some of the answers to questions I was unable to find at my school, but still it was very limited.

Has anything changed due to the celebration of a month of Black history? I for one don't see much change. I would ask why thousands of years of history is condensed into a single month. The rich history of Black people throughout the world and the contribution we have made is loosely documented and sometimes forgotten or worse anglicised. The school curriculum has not changed enough to make my children or my grandchildren understand where and how their family originated.

The contribution that Black people have made to modern society should be given equal prominence in the historical education system. Much of history is written by the conquerors that wiped out the culture of the losing nation. The influences of Black history are everywhere;

music, buildings, science, in the foods we eat, to the clothes we wear, but yet the origins of those influences are subtlety forgotten.

Times are changing slowly for Black history. From 2008 children aged between 11 and 14 are taught about the slave trade and the British Empire as part of the national history curriculum and gain an understanding of modern-day issues, especially the impact of British immigration. These subjects are designed to highlight the influence of ethnic minorities on society today and will join the two world wars and the Holocaust as periods that are compulsory parts of the history syllabus. School children are also learning about the roles of William Wilberforce, the MP who campaigned for the abolition of slavery, and Olaudah Equiano, a former slave who after buying his freedom, became an explorer and wrote his autobiography highlighting the horrors of the slave trade. Schools do have Black History Month which is the focus of most of the discussion around the Black contribution to society, but this however is not a compulsory part of the curriculum and therefore not celebrated by all schools.

Television however has led the way in promoting Black role models and encouraged the thirst for more knowledge. For example, my mixed heritage five-year old granddaughter's hero is Doc McStuffins, an animated Black female toy doctor. Consequently, she has asked my son medical questions and found out that the first person to successfully operate on twins co-joined by the back of their heads was Ben Carson, a leading Black neurosurgeon. This led to more questions and she has used the internet to find the answers rather than her school.

Black History Month has established a small legacy. However, it is still not mainstreamed. October does highlight what we have achieved as pioneers against adversary and prompts the "I didn't know that" response to facts that are unearthed about our Black innovators. Black history is part of world history and should not be relegated to just one month. I for one want recognition of the contribution of Black culture in its many forms to be highlighted in the life we lead today.

Doc McStuffins from the episode *"Rescue Ronda, Ready for Takeoff"*

ACTIVISTS

LOST LEGENDS 30 YEARS 30 VOICES

IRIS LIGHTFOOTE

BLACK HISTORY MONTH: ITS VALUE AND SIGNIFICANCE

To fully appreciate the relevance of Black History Month, we must be clear of its meaning and its purpose. Too often individuals become involved in situations and circumstances because they believe they must be seen to be in the mix to show they are appropriate, before determining the appropriateness of the situation. For some (to include institutions) that involvement is restricted to the dates ascribed to the month and absolutely no attention is paid to the topic beyond the end date.

How many of us as a result of attending a Black History Month event do anything to expand our knowledge before the following year's season and, for those who will be attending for the first time, how many will do any research prior to attending? It is important to not only ensure learning is derived from the season but an understanding of how to use that learning:

> *"A race of people is like an individual man; until it uses its own talent, takes pride in its own history, expresses its own culture, affirms its own selfhood, it can never fulfil itself."*

Malcolm X (El-Hajj Malik El-Shabazz, 1964)

Black History Month is to honour the past achievements and on-going contributions made by people of African descent. It is about reconnecting with the past to help shape the positive future. But how can this be, if we restrict that involvement to the designated month and do nothing in between to expand that knowledge and experience?

> *"The events which transpired five thousand years ago; five years ago or five minutes ago, have determined what will happen five minutes from now; five years from now and five thousand years from now. All history is a current event."*

Dr. John Henrik Clarke (1967)

It should be understood that the full involvement in Black history, be it contained within a season, a month or a week, will undoubtedly prevent death of the mind as

> *"...the person who is in mental bondage will be 'self-contained.' ...not only will that person fail to challenge beliefs and patterns of thought which control him, he will defend and protect those beliefs and patterns of thought virtually with his last dying effort."*

Asa G Hilliard III (1988)

Carter Godwin Woodson (1875-1950), a son of former slaves who later became an author, journalist and historian, realised

> *"When you control a man's thinking you do not have to worry about his actions. You do not have to tell him to stand here or go yonder. He will find his 'proper place' and will stay in it. You do not need to send him to the back door. He will go without being told. In fact, if there is no back door, he will cut one for his special benefit. His education makes it necessary."*

Carter Godwin Woodson (1933)

28

Woodson launched Negro History Week, a precursor of Black History Month, in February 1926.

The mis-education of Black people is not restricted to America. The London Strategic Policy Unit, as part of the African Jubilee year declaration launch in 1987, established the annual event 'Black History Month'. Akyaaba Addai Sebbo, an officer in the Greater London Council (GLC) is regarded as the person who established Black History Month in England. The first event was held on 1 October 1987, and was attended by Dr Maulana Karenga, the originator of Kwanzaa (part of a cultural and spiritual programme that takes place every December), on the invitation of the GLC. The declaration called on the need for recognition of African contributions to all areas of life in the UK to include cultural, religious, economic and political (Vernon, 2013).

Critics suggest it is insulting to relegate this very important history to a month, suggesting that Black history is (World) history and should be seen as such.

Mia Morris (2011) responded thus:

> *"In an ideal world, the month would not be necessary because educational establishments and the national curriculum would fully recognise and appreciate the contribution of Black people throughout history. The Black community uses the season as an opportunity to demonstrate pride in its creativity, respect for its intellectual prowess, and a celebration of its cultural identity which is far too often misrepresented, when it is not being ignored in the mainstream."*

It is the aforementioned which has been at the forefront of The Race Equality Centre's (TREC) rationale of its involvement and contribution to Black history programmes. This contribution over the years has been located within the overarching context of the manner within which the organisation delivers its work: using the personal, cultural and social principles of exploring and addressing racism is integral to all areas of its delivery. One element of this contribution is the delivery or facilitation of public debates which have included for example:

- Black people and British politics
- Black arts - artists and representation
- Black protest and resistance to oppression
- The hidden history of Black rugby players in Britain
- Black voices in social policy development
- Chronology of Black women organising in Britain
- We were all there (WW1)
- Remembering the contributions made (WW1)
- The failure of race equality over 30 years
- Political representation and race equality
- Ethnic minorities and coaching in elite level football in England
- Race discrimination in employment: 'double jeopardy' for racial minority women

29

The topic(s), rather than being a means of extolling the key note speaker(s), was calculatingly delivered to ensure a curiosity and a quest for more knowledge from the audience. TREC use other mediums to share knowledge, including publishing articles, developing touring exhibitions, facilitating seminars and providing direction for those working with young people.

In order to fight against the airbrushing of a people and their nations from the minds, there is an obligation placed on those who know, to share knowledge with those who do not. This should begin to bring a balance to a situation of a people whose history (in the main) is at worst absent from the regularly used text books or worst still, misrepresented within said books.

"What became of the Black people of Sumer?
The traveller asked the old man.
For, ancient records show that the
people of Sumer were Black.
What happened to them?
Ah, the old man sighed.
They lost their history, so they died."

Dr. Chancellor Williams (1974)

Black Nationalist leader and Nation of Islam spokesman Malcolm X in Oxford with Eric Abrahams, right, the Student Union president, before addressing university students on the subject of extremism and liberty *(3 December 1964)*. Photograph by Keystone/Hulton Archive/Getty Images.

31

COM-MU-NITY

32

Pamela Campbell-Morris, *Carnival Queen (1986)*.

LOST LEGENDS 30 YEARS 30 VOICES

COMMUNITY

PAMELA CAMPBELL-MORRIS

BLACK HISTORY MONTH 365 DAYS

Black history should not just be a month, it should be all year round and embedded into our everyday activities. Black history is important for all of us, for ourselves, for our children. Here in England it is not known, Black history is not taught in schools so it is down to the parents, it is down to the grandparents, to the community and community groups to ensure that our Black history stays alive for our children, grandchildren and the wider community.

I was born in Gloucester, and raised in Jamaica, before returning to England at the grand old age of 16. I did some further education in Gloucester before moving to Leicester, where I started my nursing training and I've been in Leicester ever since. I must admit I wasn't involved that much with communities when I first came to Leicester, I was just finding my feet, but in 1986 I entered the Carnival Queen completion and won (I was again crowned Queen in 1989, the first person to win in Leicester twice) and that was when my real involvement became active, in Leicester, and in the community. I started putting on troupes to involve more people in carnival, not just here in Leicester; Leeds, Birmingham, Nottingham, Preston, Manchester and Derby. I also work with individuals to build their confidence and self-esteem and support them to particpate in entering the Queen, Prince, Princess, Mama and Papa competitions. I also run the Bumpa Crew which has troupe members from toddlers right up to 90 years old.

I was the project manager of the Ajani Women and Girls Centre for a number of years. Many of our projects were to educate young girls and their parents about Black history, and involve them and inform them about our great inventors and creators, people that are not taught about in school, and the Caribbean side of Black history. There was a lady called Carol Griffiths who was very inspirational in organising a programme of activities, a very different programme of activities because Ajani Women and Girls Centre was a very African centric organisation that really strived on Black history throughout the year. As Black history was not taught in schools, it was very important as an organisation to ensure that it was very much at the top of the agenda.

On the school wall where I was brought up in Jamaica it says "not for school we learn, but for life" and this is so true. The name of an independent group that I work for at the African Caribbean Centre now is called the Community Learning Project (CLIP), and got its name from this saying. It is my belief that we continue to learn and we are always learning from each other, we are never too old to learn and we are never too young to teach, so it is important for us to continue doing that, to continue in our conversations so we recognise where we are coming from and the good work we have done. Within the Community Learning Group on a weekly basis Black history is part of our conversation for us to pass that on so it remains and passes on from on from generation to generation and ensures Black history is at the forefront of our minds.

Leicester is very renowned for putting on a lot of Black history events and for us it is important to encourage people to go along and participate, listen. We have had a few very high profile speakers and spoken word artists, writers, poets, and that it's important to get involved. I would like to see more funding being put into community groups so we can have speakers coming in, talking about Black history and getting more grassroots people involved, who probably would not have otherwise engaged. I would love very much to see a mix across generations participating in Black History Month.

To ensure that we are reaching out to people Black History Month needs to be right across the city, not just one organisation, not just one setting, building on what we've done the year previously. There is a lot of talent here in Leicester in the performing arts, who can take messages across to people who would not normally listen to other people. We need to use those people as a vehicle to bring more people to the forefront who would not normally engage with Black History Month. We need different layers, from the renowned people to the grassroots and the opportunity to mix, that's the only way, as the words say 'each one, teach one'. That will inspire people to take the words of Black history and the message of Black history further into the community, deeper into the grassroots community, that is really key.

I've got a passion in ensuring that messages are getting out to the African Caribbean community. I'm also involved with the Centre for BME Health. We are well known for not attending events and participating, but I would say I'm doing my best in ensuring that people are being more receptive to engagement and participating, getting involved. Whether it's attending events or performing, we need to have different faces, new faces.

We also need to document more. I don't know if we think that we are going to be living forever but I know for example that within the African Caribbean community, we have lost so many good memories and things that could have been archived. The great Wolde Selassie, they used to call him the walking dictionary, he had so much information. Wolde was a great guy, a big smile every time you saw him. There was nothing you couldn't ask that man, he was like a walking encyclopaedia,

you just had to listen to him. He was very warm, welcoming, he was just someone that everybody was warmed to, he was very, very loved and he loved people, he loved his culture and he did it with a passion, with great pride, it's a shame we've lost a great man. Raddle Books as well. From the outside it was just a little shop but if you looked through the window, you could see that it represents African Caribbean people, because the flags that were in the window or books that you could see from outside. It would draw you in and it was very welcoming. You could walk into that shop and you just got to look around and the whole shop I could see someone that looks like me, so even if I didn't buy a book, the fact that they had Black staff was very important. Quite a lot of the books as well, my children have had books from there and it was great, you'd think 'wow, there's a picture of a Black woman looks like my grandma, there's a picture of a man that looks like my dad'. I do believe visuals are as important as words.

When I speak to the older generation, just on a one to one, some of the times I wish I had a recorder to capture those memories. We just need to find a way of harnessing it, of capturing it in its raw sense because that is a legacy that can be passed on from generation to generation.

My final word is Black history is great. We have a lot of reasons to continue to celebrate and to make Black history even greater.

34

DOROTHY FRANCIS

NO BIG DEAL

Black History Month divides my loyalties and fosters a duality of pleasure and resentment within me. I love theatre, dance, poetry, readings and debate so revel in the opportunity to satiate myself on a month long culture festival. I am a consumer of arts rather than a creator and am in awe of the huge outpouring of talent that is Black History Month. But at the same time I feel like a binge eater greedily shovelling in as much as I can during a very short window before the treats are whisked away from me again. There is a sense of feast and famine; eleven months without and then an embarrassment of riches for thirty-one days. Of course it is not so wholly cut and dried; a city like Leicester has much to offer and I acknowledge that I am able to see Black artists and performers all year round, albeit in less dense concentration.

My discontent stems from the fact that I believe that every month should be Black History Month. Why is our culture confined to a showcase of a few weeks per year? Can one single month contain the outpouring of art, culture, inventions and talent that are the contribution of people of African descent? Carter G Woodson, the African-American historian who originally promoted the idea that became Black History Month hoped that one day the need to have such a celebration would prove unnecessary as Black people would be so integrated into society that it would not be necessary to single out our achievements in a bid to ensure that we are afforded equality of recognition. However, I would argue that we are a long way from that ideal and acknowledge that perhaps without Black History Month the contributions of people of African descent would be neglected even further.

Black History Month celebrates the men and women who have changed - and continue to change - the world that we live in and I fully support the spotlight that the month shines on Black scientists, inventors, doctors, artists, explorers and reformers and the way that Black success is promoted by organisations such as Serendipity through a range of media including music, dance and drama. But how do people of African descent find out about their history when every day is white history day but Black history is confined to an annual festival? How do they learn that Black women calculated the maths that put men on the moon? That Charles Drew developed the technology to establish blood banks, thus saving millions of lives? Or that Claudia Jones founded the UK's first major Black newspaper, The West Indian Gazette, in 1958, bringing the concerns of Black people to the fore at a time when many establishments displayed signs proclaiming "No Blacks, no Irish, no dogs"?

How can children learn of their history in an accessible way when most significant contributions of people of African descent are absent from text books? The National Curriculum defends the importance of learning history because "It supports pupils to develop their own identities and it helps them to ask and answer questions of the present by engaging in the past". But this can only be effective if history holds up a mirror that equally reflects the past of all cultures and ethnicities. Many children of African descent do not see themselves in history books except for the toe-curling embarrassment of lessons about slavery. As the only Black child in my class how well I remember the taunting and bullying that followed those lessons and my sense of deep anger that

36

Claudia Jones at the National Communist Headquarters in New York, *(26 January 1948)*.
Photograph by Hulton Archive/Getty Images.

the only mirror held up to me throughout my time at school was one that reflected slavery whilst ignoring all positive aspects of my culture.

On leaving school I was able to recite Shakespeare, list Henry VIII's wives and describe the topography of the Yorkshire Dales, but had never heard of Nanny of the Maroons, Queen Nzinga, or the great walls of Zimbabwe. I didn't know that Africans sailed to America hundreds of years before Columbus or that the largest library of the ancient world was on African soil. I learned Black history through a process of searching for facts and evidence (not easy in a pre-internet age), painstakingly piecing together evidence through research, debates, and lectures. My friends and I formed a group called The Descendants of Africa to promote Black culture through discussion, music, dance and food and formed a partnership with Coventry Cathedral where we could be found most weekends outreaching to visitors through food and conversation. I followed Alice Walker's advice and learned to read books "not for facts but for clues" and used these clues to progress into other areas of discovery. I travelled to London to attend Sunday afternoon sessions at New Beacon Books where I listened to speakers from across the diaspora who introduced me to wider spheres of knowledge. My friends and I established a Black bookshop called Radix, which means "the root", because we wanted to get back to the roots of our history and culture. This piecing together eventually formed a rich cultural tapestry that allowed me to understand and celebrate my uniqueness and place in the world as an individual of African heritage but it was hard fought for and that fight should not have been necessary.

I enjoy celebrating Black History Month in Leicester and have attended some amazing events. Highlights over the years have been Jean Binta Breeze's Creative Salon, Michelle Vacciana's intriguing show 'Journey Cakes' and the opening event of the 2015 festival, 'Strange Fruit: A Tribute to Billie Holiday' which afforded an opportunity to dress up in 1950s vintage clothing. There have been events outside October such as Urban Bush Women, who performed as part of Let's Dance International Frontiers in 2016, and proved once again why this dance company is one of the best in the world. Another favourite is the annual Gospel Showcase which always causes the audience to leave with a smile on their faces.

I am happy that we are developing our own cultural icons in the UK and that we don't need to gaze across the pond to find inspiration. Writers such as Jean Binta Breeze, Kerry Young and Jacob Ross have made their homes in Leicester and tell stories that are seen through a Black British perspective rather than a white gaze. Andrea Levy, Courttia Newland, Jackie Kay and Malorie Blackman write of essentially British themes whilst Black British actors such as Naomie Harris and Idris Elba straddle the UK and USA with ease. They are helping to form what I like to call a 'no big deal' diversity whereby their work is accepted simply as art rather than 'Black art'. Black History Month is a worthwhile concept but its work will be done when it is no longer needed because the contribution of Black people is so fully integrated and accepted that it is truly No Big Deal.

Michelle Vacciana in *Journey Cakes (2013)*

DONNA JACKMAN

NOBODY, NOBODY OWNS BLACK HISTORY MONTH

In my opinion, nobody owns Black History Month, nobody owns the concept, but as we all know the concept came from America. As a child growing up I witnessed the Civil Rights Movement watching television as the issue of racial oppression in the UK had not hit the television screens but the American situation resonated with us in Britain.

What was happening in America was slightly different from what was happening in Britain but as that generation was growing up, compared to our parents' generation and with technology development, we had more of an understanding of what was happening. America also introduced us to a wealth of literature that was coming from Black writers, African Americans talking about the Civil Rights Movement, talking about Blackness, talking about people of colour, talking about people's rights, and as a generation I think that really caught our imagination. Black History Month was born out of the new wave of writers and thinking and one of the reasons for the concept of having a season was it allowed us time to focus on ourselves, who we are as a people. So that's where Black history started for me, and I think many other people in Leicester.

Leicester wasn't like London; Black History Month didn't start as a national movement. It came to the Black communities at different times, it started where there were Black activists in the community, and political activists who saw Black history and the amazing concept where we could look at our pasts legitimately, and not apologise. There wasn't a national cohesion, people started to organise events in Nottingham, Leicester, Manchester; wherever Black people were and could have been on a big scale or on a much smaller scale.

As a Black pupil, I was aware of discrimination in Britain, because of my day to day experience and because of Britain's involvement with the slave trade. Shame is not a part of the British memory, people had forgotten but there is also a sense of denial in terms of the impact that the slave trade had, and is still having, on Black people in America, the Caribbean and the UK. It didn't matter what school you went to because, at the time, you knew if you challenged the teachers and their concept of the Black people, people of African descent, you were immediately slapped down and reminded that you didn't know what you were talking about.

Later on, when we had access to Black academic information, we had the tools and the confidence to find the words to challenge this.

I think, opposition to this denial is at the heart of why Black History Month was created. We wanted to learn for ourselves, because we didn't trust anything that mainstream education and media was telling us. With the development of Black academics in America we were able to have a better view of that history and a more truthful view of that history which made us angry and upset, but at the same time gave us an opportunity to start developing a sense of pride of who we are and who we can be in the future.

Leicester Black History Month activities started on a fairly small scale, of those of us who were active coming together and saying 'have you read this book, have you read that book?' and sharing that information. Raddle Books started with Wolde Selassie, who passed away a few years ago. He used to have a bookshop in a suitcase,

TELEPHONE 24875

Specialists in African, Caribbean & African-American books, arts, crafts & records.

40

Small Selection
ROOTS MUSIC
(available)

ALARM

numbers

Raddle Books. Photographer Earle Robinson, reproduced with permission of Leicester City Council.

ADDLE
BOOKS

he literally used to go to events with a suitcase and he would open his suitcase and he would have these books that people wanted to buy because they were not accessible. We couldn't get these books in the libraries, they were not available in the bookshops, most of these books came from America and later the Caribbean. Raddle Books was crucial in providing that opportunity to be able to buy culturally specific books offering a broader perspective. The suitcase became an actual bookshop in Highfields and we used to meet in the backroom to discuss what we had read, early days of what is now fashionably called a 'book club'. These meetings led to doing events on a very small, very local level with a few people, without the local authority support or intervention. It wasn't funded, it was about the excitement of discovery and learning and understanding we had a greater contribution to history than we first perceived and that we continue to contribute as a people. There were other community organisations coming to the forefront such as Spectrum and Ajani Women and Girls Centre, of which Carol Leeming and I were founder members. For many people that was a key moment in time when we started linking up with people in London, but it was largely individuals such as Wolde Selassie, Carol Leeming and myself taking the lead with organising. We were involved in African Caribbean Education, a Saturday school which was developed from the previous generation for children to supplement Black children's education, covering Black history that was not taught in schools and to support them. Institutional racism has a big impact, failing large numbers of Black children. Some parents were working two jobs, they had to put food on the table, they had to pay the rent, and they didn't often have the opportunity to sit down with their children. One of the reasons why people left the

41

Caribbean was to try and create a better life and get an education, no different to the migrants coming to Britain today.

Leicester African Caribbean Arts Forum (LACAF) was an organisation that was created to look at arts and culture, to empower Black people in the arts, and to support local artists whatever their discipline. LACAF embraced Black History Month and started organising events at Moat Community College, and this is where Black History Month became more exclusively focused on the arts. I was a Chair of LACAF for a while and it was that organisation I think who started looking at funding, both from the local authority and independently.

One of the big things for us was to organise family fun days, with the idea of that intergenerational coming together of parents, children, grandparents, aunts, uncles. Providing fun and a lot of our events took place at Moat Community College, where we'd charge little amounts of money as a way of fundraising. We would start off with libation, thanking the ancestors for the fact that we're here now, and we'd have storytelling, arts and cultural activities, traditional board games, African music, things like the Kora and drumming, which have always been central in all of our activities as, the drums are used to call people together. It is really about that collective understanding, collective knowledge of our cultural past. It is very important for Black children to foster that sense of pride. I think if you were to only listen to what schools said you'd learn nothing, so getting schools to see Black history as a really positive thing and having the family fun days were really, really important.

Then organisations such as De Montfort University, De Montfort Hall, the Haymarket started to become more involved in Black History Month. There was pressure on them, I suppose, to get involved and put on events and the programme became broader. Wolde was centrally involved in the development of Black History Month in this city and he was doing some work at New Walk Museum and found lots of African artefacts we didn't even know were there. There was an exhibition where all of these creative Black people in the city got together, and from those objects weaved stories around them. The idea was that you take the objects and you tell a story, it was a spiritual story, a journey and we actually developed the museum inside and out, obviously, if you're looking at a traditional African event it's not inside, everything's outside. That was an amazing event. I think we amazed ourselves really because you are curating stories, we used actual artefacts to create the stories and that's what storytelling is all about really, isn't it?

We also did something called Nubion Star Lounge at the Haymarket and that was music, spoken word, poetry and theatre. Carol Leeming wrote the play. Style Up was another event which we did at the museum, an exhibition of fashion looking at African fashion in particular. We put out a call to people to bring in photos of themselves when they were young, and to look at the sort of clothing, fashions that they were wearing. It's surprising really, but people had kept stuff from the 40s and the 50s, women in particular, and we had young Black models.

Many of us would go to other events in other cities like Nottingham, London, Manchester, Leeds so it wasn't just about Leicester but looking at what other people were doing up and down the country, and I was centrally involved in with other people like Carol, Wolde and Pawlet and other creatives in the city at the time.

I think about the question that was raised 'should Black History Month be scrapped or revamped?' whose right is it to ask that question? Who owns Black history? The times that we're in, even after 30 years, and with so little investment, but that investment is only possible if we stay invested in it because otherwise who are we doing it for? People can hide behind technology, but we will find them. We're not that generation that is going to sit back and watch that happen and do nothing because 30 years we've been fighting this. If people think that Black History Month should go, why? It's not just an academic issue for those of us who have grown up over the last 30 years, it's an emotional issue, that's our youth for many of us and that helped to define what we are today and how we feel today. But I think even if you were to get rid of Black History Month tomorrow, in 50 years it would come back again. There's always going to be a need for Black people to keep on defining who we are and not allow other people to do that for us. We do that for ourselves and what will come out of that will be activities and raising our voices.

43

Shashamane O'Neill, *Style Up Exhibition 2007,*
Reproduced with permission of Carol Leeming,
© Leicester Museums and Galleries

44

Elvy Morton at her friend's wedding ceremony in Nottingham (circa 1976).

ELVY MORTON

BLACK HISTORY MONTH THE WORLD

Over the years "Black history" has been a subject that has upset some people and also pleased some.

What is "Black history"?

To me it is world history. Black History is an on-going entity. As Black history is being researched you realise all the myths that are attached to it, through the ages how Black history is being stolen and a "white" slant is put on it. Dr Daniel Hale Williams who performed the first successful open heart surgery was the first Black American to be given a doctorate, but there are some who would not recognise his achievement so give the accolade to a white doctor in South Africa.

There are still some universities who are afraid of upsetting the privileged few so put out wrong information. What upset the majority of Black people is that Black history has only come into existence for the last 60 years. Black history was buried for a purpose because Black people were getting too big for their boots. The majority of Black Caribbean people who came to the Britain in the "Windrush era" are to this day still bemused by the fact that the British still know nothing about the Caribbean people yet the people of the Caribbean knew so much about the people of Britain.

By the way, what is this about "Black History Month"? Why a month? One only has to look back at the people of the Nile Valley to realise their achievements before western civilisation.

There were so many books of the Black Sambo type that had to be destroyed by some of us from the Caribbean to let our children know that they can be Black and proud of their forefathers' achievements. Also at the same time to encourage our young people to do their own research to get a true identity of their selves.

There are many books that can help to destroy the myths about Black history, dig them out, study them and learn about the history of the world and not just about Western history and civilisation.

A person who knows
And knows not that they know
Is asleep – awaken them
A person who knows
And knows that they know
Is wise – follow them
All of these persons reside in you
Know Thy Self

Part of an ancient proverb (in Browder, 1992)

Festac '77. Lagos, Nigeria. (15 January - 13 February, 1977). Photographer © Marilyn Nance.

FLORENCE CHANAKIRA-NYAHWA

OUR HISTORY AND OUR IDENTITY

Everybody's identity matters. It equally matters that they know it well in its truth, with its glory and blemishes. As in Jimmy Cliff's song "Who feels it knows it", history needs to be told by those who lived it and who still live its history. It also needs to be told too, by everybody, also in truth.

Leicester is privileged to have senior members in the African Heritage community, who for some of us newcomers, regard as having contributed to 'Lost Legends', in spirit and in kind, by providing us with a better understanding of the evolution of our community over the years and at various forums.

I had previously come from Africa to the United Kingdom to study, for conferences or to see family. It had never occurred to me that one day I would come back and live for a while in Leicester. My husband got a job here and a year later I came to join him. This was at the time when I was laying down the foundation of our African international organisation which works for better education across cultures and people of difference which we named the S M Nyahwa Foundation (SMNF) after my husband passed on. Having grown up under apartheid and segregation in Southern Africa, this naturally is an important aspect for nation building in that part of the world, just as it is now worldwide. We work in partnership with organisations and educational institutions who have the same focus. Our activities have been based on my experiences in the USA with the African American University Women's Association, in Holland, Denmark and several African and Caribbean countries where we also have partners.

1977 was a landmark in culture of the African Heritage people worldwide. I was fortunate that while I studied in Nigeria then, I participated in the Second World Black African Festival of Arts and Culture (FESTAC'77) organised and hosted by that nation. It was quite amazing with contingents from all of Africa's nations and its diaspora. The United Kingdom was well represented. The colloquium that was scheduled during the festival drew from leading African Heritage politicians, historians, artists and scientists from all over the world, and its scope stands unparalleled. The legacy of FESTAC'77 lives on both as The Centre for Black and African Arts and Civilisation (CBAAC) based in Lagos, Nigeria and in the Conference of Intellectuals from Africa and the Diaspora Africa (CIAD). The first FESTAC had been hosted on a smaller scale by Senegal, with much inspiration from the late President Sengor, who most of us will remember for his great contribution to the discussion on 'Negritude'. As we reflect on our Lost Legends in Leicester, I would like to take this opportunity to congratulate FESTAC' 77 as it celebrates its fortieth anniversary this year and appreciate the archive of information they safeguard on our behalf.

Coming back to the SMNF, the focus of our activities are aimed at better understanding across cultures and other divides. We have a special project that focuses on Africa/Africa diaspora culture. In Leicester, we have formed partnerships with organisations with same interest as ours, and have linked up with community cohesion activities both at county and city council level, as well as with our universities and other cultural organisations. As part of the then Leicester Ethnic Minority Partnership

47

(LEMP) we networked and organised events with associations of various sectors of the African Heritage community and we were contracted by the BBC to outreach into minority communities when they switched to digital TV transmission. This was really exciting as the minority communities in Leicester are so diverse.

In partnership with Christians Aware, SMNF has a joint project called "Listen to Africa" (L2A), and we organise lectures, exhibitions, workshops and visits to Africa and the Caribbean Islands. L2A hosts an in-house annual seminar on topical issues relating to African heritage communities based here in the UK or overseas. One of the most informative lectures we have organised was with De Montfort University highlighting the evolution of multicultural Leicester. The keynote speaker from Leicester City Council's community cohesion unit gave a comprehensive and very informative presentation. One could follow the changes in diversity of the African Heritage Community and get an overall profile of multicultural Leicester.

The formation of the Leicester Black History Season consortium was a welcome development and our organisations were signatory to its setting up at the grand occasion held in the Secular Society Hall, Humberstone Gate, Leicester. The consortium had monthly meetings which were dynamic and productive and led to much networking beyond the meeting room. I wish to pay tribute to the late (Dr) Wolde Selassie for his visionary contribution and for sharing with us his wealth of knowledge in all spheres of African heritage. His last lecture at the African Caribbean Centre was on the history of mathematics in Africa. I was delighted whilst

listening to a BBC radio programme discussing a similar topic, to hear some of the information, which I got from the late Wolde's lecture. He was in contact with other African Heritage organisations worldwide, so we were always abreast with events especially in Africa, the Americas and other parts of Europe.

Black History Month is part of a global invisible infrastructure connected through the journey and stories of Black people worldwide and I have welcomed the opportunity to be able to contribute to Black History Month through the development of the projects I have been involved with over the last 30 years.

SHAKHA PALMER

KNOWLEDGE OF SELF AND BLACK HISTORY MONTH

Black History Month is something which I hold very dear to my heart because it's difficult to understand who you are and where you're going without looking back and reflecting on your past. If we lose something, the best thing we can do is retrace our footsteps to a previous time or place. Even over the last thirty years, things have evolved and slowly changed with the sense of familiarity in terms of the environment you have adapted to.

I don't think I'm old enough to fully comment on my experience of 30 years of Black History Month because I've only recently started getting involved or attending events. Black History Month in my opinion should be celebrated first and foremost by the African Caribbean Community, for the African Caribbean Community but how is that now possible within such a diverse community? Black history is not commonly taught in schools in England and if they are able to teach some topics they will only focus on the usual periods in time such as slavery or famine in Ethiopia.

Black History Month is an opportunity to encourage the young African Caribbean/Mixed Heritage community to learn about some of their history that they may be unaware of. We live in a time where some young people are struggling to cope with their own identity because they have been told very little information about who they are and where they come from. We currently live in a very conservative society where period dramas appear to be the in thing, but period dramas are very rarely based on Black ancestry. The more period dramas about Black people you have the opportunity to watch, the more you will become accustomed to your past and be more confident in who you are.

Many people have raised concerns about people who struggle to find knowledge of self because they are unaware of the reason behind why they are struggling; it could end up potentially being an historic systemic problem. African Americans are still unfortunately lynched and hung by the neck in some states of America but we all know that this is nothing new, it is historic. Slaves transported from Africa to America taught their children about their African heritage because they knew that their culture would be lost over time. The 'Black Panther Party' also saw Black history as an important part of their movement because they were so passionate about the importance of seeking knowledge of self.

I grew up in a society where Black role models were scarce and I was constantly bombarded with actors, news reporters and television presenters that I struggled to identify with. Black history was something I had not been introduced to because nobody seemed to talk about it in my social circle at that particular period in time. Not being able to connect with my past must have had an impact on my mental wellbeing and I must have portrayed some signs of uncertainty. The first book I read on the subject of Black history was the biography of Malcolm X written by Alex Haley. I couldn't believe that there was somebody who shared some of the same frustrations as me. Once I had completed the biography I became passionate about Black activism and the history of the Black power movement in America. I quickly began to become curious about the economic advantages and disadvantages of the Trans-Atlantic Slave Trade.

50

View of a line of Black Panther Party members as they stand outside the New York City courthouse. *(11 April 1969).* Photograph by David Fenton/Getty Images.

Black History Month has also given Black artists a platform to express their talent and introduce themselves to a wider audience, which is vital in an industry where it is becoming harder to break through. I think it is important to celebrate the arts because music, dance and theatre are a major part of Black culture, they should be celebrated. Black History Month over the years has presented a variety of local and national talent at venues and events across the city of Leicester; music and entertainment always seems to be a big winner.

I have only ever really explored three Black History Months and I have to say that I've been very impressed with most of the events I have attended, but there is room for more. Unfortunately, there has always been mixed views on how Black History Month should be organised, which has led people to exclude themselves from the project altogether. To be able to continue celebrating this important month of the year I think that people need to see Black History Month as a celebration again, rather than a project, and get involved.

I have personally gained a lot of knowledge and experience from the few Black History Months that I have managed to attend and I look forward to celebrating a few more. I think that we should be encouraging this generation to leave a legacy for the next generation. Unity is also definitely an important factor in the overall success of the month and the African Caribbean Community has to put their differences aside or deliver their own projects. I really do think that it's important that more young people are able to get involved through different channels that are easily accessible through community groups and school programmes.

I personally think that Black History Month will always be celebrated in some way, shape or form but we should always read about our history so we know exactly where we came from and where we plan on going.

I think that the local authority should invest more money into Black History Month because it has become a historical part of Leicester's history. Less and less money seems to be available for community projects and events which means that the event organisers must feel the pressure of making a small budget stretch so far. Despite the fact that funding streams are diminishing, we have still been able to enjoy a more inclusive Black History Month, packed with a variety of events. My final thoughts are that there should be more academic events that focus on studies carried out by Black lecturers and leading experts. This would help to reposition Black History Month in schools and in the curriculum and be part of a new future that gives a more balanced historical picture.

"If the black subject and black experience are not stabilised by Nature or by some other essential guarantee, then it must be the case that they are constructed historically, culturally, politically - and the concept which refer to this is 'ethnicity'.**"**

Stuart Hall (1998)

BRIAN SIMMONDS

THE DEATH OF BLACK HISTORY MONTH

I will begin by naming a few things that impacted on the African heritage community (AHC) - people of African origin and who are influenced by the place and the people around them in the UK, from Black Lives Matter campaign to the first degree course in Black Studies starting in 2017 at Birmingham City University.

We were all witness to a deluge of programmes on traditional television primarily on BBC throughout October and November 2016 (Black History Month Season) celebrating the impact of the AHC contribution to British history worldwide. But how will this impact on the next generation of African Heritage young people in Britain celebrating Black History Month 2017 and beyond?

The first and most obvious thing to note is that in 2013 after 25 years Leicester City Council decided to change Black History Season (encapsulating October – November months) to Black History Month Leicester. The reason giving by the local authority was "to be in line with the rest of the UK celebrating Black History Month".

Black History Month in the UK takes place in October, rather than in February, as in the USA and many other places. I am not going to go too deeply into this scheduling issue, except to suggest that this should tell you that the whole Black History Month idea was misconceived from conception in the UK.

Black History Month is supposedly a tool for the AHC to (re) connect with their global history and yet from the very outset there was a failure to consider and co-ordinate with other AHCs around the globe who had already instituted Black History Month. This failure can perhaps be attributed to ignorance, parochialism or the control of non-AHC funders.

If you live in the UK you may have noticed the steady, and in the last few years, dramatic, decline of Black History Month events in your community. The problem with Black History Month in the UK is that its creation and funding was in complete contradiction to the principles and values it was meant to promote. That is to say from very early in its development it became dependent upon funding from the local authorities. So we had a people who were seeking to reclaim their history and culture for the purpose of (and this is the bit that is so often forgotten, ignored or not even understood) exercising self-deterministic power in the world, going 'cap in hand' (yes that's where the word handicapped comes from) to their historical and contemporary conquerors for the money to teach their community how to become liberated!!

> *"History shows that it does not matter who is in power...those who have not learned to do for themselves and have to depend solely on others never obtain any more rights or privileges in the end than they had in the beginning."*
>
> Dr Carter G Woodson (1933)

The above quote from Carter G Woodson the progenitor of what we now call Black History Month/African History Month/African History Season gets right to the nub of why he created Negro History Week and the purpose it was meant to serve. The (re)learning, remembrance and celebration of African history was meant to be purposive and that purpose was to assist in moving the sons and daughters of Africa from their then (and now) position of oppression under an invidious racial caste system created by Caucasians, to a position of power, self-sufficiency and dignity.

Jamaican born African-American nationalist Marcus Garvey *(1887 - 1940)*, *the founder of the Universal Negro Improvment Association (UNIA)*. Photograph by MPI/Getty Images.

So Black History Month in the UK was placed upon the auction block right from the beginning and sold to the only bidder; the local authority. We are all familiar with the saying 'he who pays the piper calls the tune' and it became very clear that the white payer wanted the Black piper to play songs entitled 'Rainbow coalition', 'Multiculturalism', 'Diversity', 'Sing and Dance 'til your feet hurt', 'Forget Economics, we're Black', 'Power is a dirty word' and other diversionary hits. As time went on they got tired of this Black equals African idea and wanted everyone to get under the bastardised BME umbrella and to celebrate diversity.

The AHC were asked to prostitute themselves (and by extension us) for local authority funding. God forbid the AHC actually funded our own cultural celebrations. With the funding came the political imperatives and in some places I have been told even the Asian community get in on the Black History Month act!

The endemic global failure of Africans to practice 'ethno-aggregation'/Ujamaa/Co-operative economics/ Powernomics, call it what you will has had profound ramifications, of which the death of Black History Month is just a minor casualty. The values and behaviours required to have independently institutionalised Black History Month in African communities across Britain are the values and behaviours required to have created a solid economic foundation in those same communities. The failure to achieve the latter ensured the failure to do the former.

We must look at the lessons that history teaches us. We must understand the tremendous value of the study of history for the re-gaining of power. If our education is not about gaining real power, we are being mis-educated and misled and will die "educated" and misled...the study of history cannot.

I have just finished reading the book 'Forty Million Dollar Slaves - The Rise, Fall and Redemption of the Black Athlete' (by William C. Rhoden) which I would highly recommend. The recurring theme throughout this book is that it does not matter how many highly paid superstar athletes we have produced, without group co-operation, loyalty and a sense of collective mission they remain powerless multi-millionaire 'slaves' dependent upon their billionaire owners. Every day we make African history, for better or worse, so the death of Black History Month is an opportunity to free the history of African people from a thirty one day (or twenty eight day) prison and liberate it to occupy the highlands and lowlands of July, January, March etc.! Far better if we commemorated special days throughout the year, for example, Marcus Mosiah Garvey's birth anniversary and Kwanzaa as high points in a constant reinforcement of our identity and culture.

So, rest in peace Black History Month, make every day African History Day.

GREGORY SMITH

'WE HAVE NOTHING TO FEAR FOR THE FUTURE EXCEPT WHERE WE FORGET OUR PAST'

'Developing Gospel arts' is a byline that Kainé uses to describe its work. It was the centrepiece that created a voluntary management organisation in 2002 and which grew into a charity by 2012. Kainé means *new life or new creation*. The organisation's efforts have supported the development of an audience base beyond the 'traditional' Black African demographic. Its evolution and progression has continued through vision, and creating new opportunity. Kainé manages five community choirs: Kainé Gospel Choir, Leicester Women's Gospel Choir, Curve Gospel Choir, Rothley Gospel Choir and Curve Junior Choir. The choir has supported the establishment and development of De Montfort University Students Choir, Leicester University (LUV) Choir and the Holy Cross community choirs. Our achievements are not just marked by events but more importantly experiences. We pride ourselves on being able to create warm, encouraging environments for people from a non-musical or non-gospel background on being able to participate and have fun!

We have always had a close relationship with Black History Month; it has assisted in defining our work in Gospel arts within the community. We have been operating for the past 15 years navigating our course through the 'highs and lows' that charities face. Our work, particularly in the early days, was sometimes misunderstood and considered *'something for the Black people on a Sunday'*. I remember a senior officer in 'arts' commenting that it was too 'in your face'. However, Gospel arts is unapologetic, vibrant, and 'in your face' because it seeks to inspire, motivate, and encourage its listeners. A refusal of a grant because we were 'promoting religion' was also successfully challenged. Rather than get upset we saw this as another opportunity to

be understood. The Black experience does not fit neatly into the established ideologies so we have been, as you have to be, prepared to 'push' to be 'heard' and understood.

The history of Gospel music has an important juxtaposition with the slave trade, the civil rights movement in the United States, apartheid in South Africa, and the numerous cries for freedom around the world. Gospel music sits against this background exciting the masses in exhilarating chorus, pulsating rhythms and percussion and bass. Black History Month provides a platform and an opportunity to share a message, a tradition, a culture and a sound.

The contributions to Black History Month through our community choir performances at our Festival of Choirs Showcase (now in its seventh year) have helped to proliferate Gospel arts beyond the traditional audience set. We take the opportunity to widen the awareness with children and young people offering Gospel arts singing workshops at schools, revisiting a younger generation with the old themes and songs but reviving them (as Gospel does) with a contemporary sound.

There are those who would say why have a season? or a month? Or a day, to celebrate Black history? I respond by saying *'we have nothing to fear for the future except where we forget our past'*. How we understand our history helps us to reflect and define our perceptions and attitudes towards each other now. How do we understand each other, if we do not recognise each other's contributions. This melting pot that is Britain after all should reflect who I am and my Black British experience; it is just as important to share and 'sing about' and recognise as any other.

The fact that we do something to celebrate and acknowledge Black History Month is important. I reflect on a time growing up when Black history was really only explored at home, church, community meetings through the discussions with elderly folk. You might get a fleeting glimpse of a Black actor on television, although every Black person of my era remembers 'Roots'. Funk or reggae artists on 'Top of the Pops' offered little more, but Black history was in the background as was ethnicity when I was very young. Black History Month was never mentioned to my knowledge let alone celebrated. Carnival was the biggest expression of sharing Black heritage. It allowed everyone to participate. We still have far to go, and I would hope we would arrive at a place when Black History Month is embedded more within education, arts, and it is championed by all. I have enjoyed the opportunity that Black history has given to showcase 'gospel arts'. I refer to embedding Black history and heritage as I believe this needs to be more than just an event, but rather an enriching experience that connects with everyone. Young Black people need Black History Month to explore who they are, rebut the negative stereotypes that society continues to churn out and everyone else deserves to know the contributions and the struggle for equality that still exists today. I would hope that in the future we can see a Black History Month which happens, by that I mean it's not a struggle to convince anyone of the argument to celebrate or hold it, I hope we move way past that discussion. I hope that it is an integrated celebration as St George's Day.

57

Singer Mahalia Jackson singing at Shrine Auditorium.
Photograph by Don Cravens/The LIFE Images Collection/Getty Images.

DIANNE VAN-DER-WESTHUIZEN

PAYING THE PRICE

My family emigrated to England in 1965 in search of a better life from South Africa. We moved to Leicester in 1968 when Black History Month did not exist. Our history was given to us by our parents it was not taught in mainstream education. What Black people were experiencing in every walk of life was a topic of conversation in Black homes across the UK, from the civil rights movement to apartheid. Leicester was a culturally diverse city, there was a mix of Caribbeans, Africans, Polish, Italians, Greeks and Asians. Leicester was a hot spot in terms of entertainment i.e. music and theatre. However, we as Black people were made to feel inferior because of the colour of our skin and our features. My brother and I were told we had to work harder than our counterparts at school to achieve because of the colour of our skin. If we did not achieve and do well at school the teachers were not particularly interested, they were more willing to push Black children towards sport. There were no Black teachers at the schools I attended, there were no Black people in popular TV shows, or in adverts. In the 1980s Saturday schools were set up to help our children to improve educationally and Black history was included from an African Caribbean perspective. Our children need to understand, appreciate and know their cultural heritage; they need to be aware of the sacrifices and achievements our ancestors made for us. Knowledge is power, and this will empower our young people, as power is wealth but it depends on how you use it.

In April 1990 Nelson Mandela was released from prison; he was imprisoned because he believed white and Black are equal regardless of the colour of our skins and this was against the principles of apartheid. I remember I was so proud to be African, especially South African, my brother was in Johannesburg and he said the atmosphere was euphoric. The people did not sleep, they were celebrating, as this signalled the end of the apartheid regime, of better times to come, of a fairer society. Nelson Mandela's time in prison did not change him into an angry and bitter person; he was compassionate, forgiving and humble.

"Education is the most powerful weapon we can use to change the world"

Nelson Mandela (2003)

Leicester honoured this great man by naming one of the central parks after him. About this time I had the pleasure of having African neighbours who had spent time in South Africa, we had common ground, we enjoyed sharing experiences and enjoyed the same music. For me this was my African experience in Leicester even though it was for a short time.

I feel over the last twenty years there has been a disconnect between Black British people and their history; this is in part to do with the rise in mixed heritage children. They do not see themselves as Black. However, I do believe if you are not white you are Black and this has never changed. Also there has been an increase in dysfunctional families. Black fathers have abdicated responsibility for their children, leaving sole parents to be responsible for providing children with their needs. Extended families no longer exist as we knew it; sole parenting whether it be fathers or mothers are having to balance the pressures of working life, childcare and spending quality time with their children. Priorities today seem to be giving children what they want and not what they need and as such our children are being starved of knowledge, their Black heritage in particular. Nothing has actually changed in this country since I arrived in the 60s. We are still being judged by the colour of our skin and the way we look. Our children are going to pay the price for this lack of knowledge, as they are not equipped.

In 2006, Jesse Jackson came to the Peepul Centre in Leicester. I was made aware of his visit by Pawlet Brookes and felt it was an opportunity not to be missed. I arranged time off from work and attended this event with my 9-year old daughter. The atmosphere was incredible; he spoke with such passion, just to be in his presence was amazing.

"Your children need your presence more than your presents"
Jesse Jackson (cited in Dunlap, 2004)

In 2016 I had the opportunity to attend the opening of Black History Month in Leicester and was entertained by Soweto Kinch. I felt uplifted as I have known this young man since he was thirteen and I felt so proud to be part of the audience, as he is an accomplished saxophonist. Black History Month includes the talents of Black people across the diaspora; I believe that Black history should be included in mainstream education,
but until this happens I think we should continue to support Black History Month.

59

"It is not our diversity which divides us; it is not our ethnicity, or religion or culture that divides us. Since we have achieved our freedom, there can only be one division amongst us: between those who cherish democracy and those who do not.**"**

Nelson Mandela

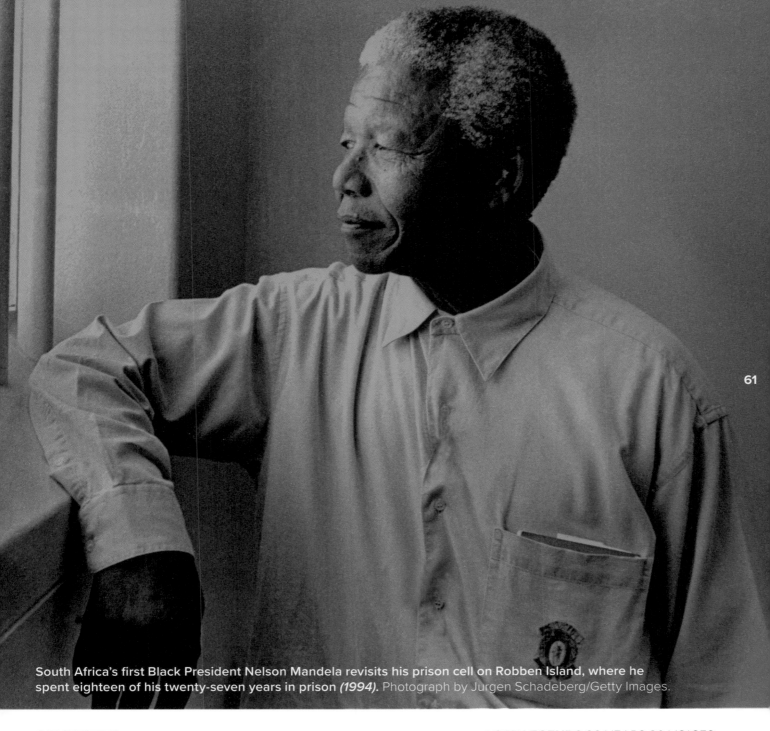

South Africa's first Black President Nelson Mandela revisits his prison cell on Robben Island, where he spent eighteen of his twenty-seven years in prison *(1994).* Photograph by Jurgen Schadeberg/Getty Images.

62

Freedom Tariq Zampaladous at Witham Villa Equestrian Centre.

FREEDOM TARIQ ZAMPALADUS

LEICESTER'S 30 YEAR LOVE AFFAIR

30 years of Black History Month in Leicester. What does this mean to me? Wow that's a serious question. I will attempt to answer this as best I can. Obviously this piece is in no way influenced by anybody else, it's my perspective and interpretation with regards to 'Leicester's 30 year love affair'.

The meaning of Black History Month means different things for different people. It's a term celebrated worldwide and dogged in controversy in equal measure.

Personally, in terms of my opinion on the phrase... that would be determined by who I'd be discussing this with, as I believe it's a case of communicating with people on different levels.

To many people Black History Month or Season is a chance to celebrate the achievements of our present, past and future during a specific moment with each other. The chance to share some of these moments with our fellow human beings of other cultures.

On the other hand, there are those who argue Black history should be celebrated every day and not just during a particular month or season. They argue that Black History Month exploits our culture and usually focuses on negative aspects of our part in history rather than past, present and future, particularly in mainstream education.

So if you're asking me what my thoughts are I would say this...

With my immediate family, I chose not to rely on Black History Month when it comes to educating them about their history. Black Fist, Black Power is engrained within their whole lifestyle and so I would say we live Black history; by the second, by the minute, by the hour, trust me it's that deep.

Kings and queens, royalty, great inventors, speakers, leaders, high achievers, yes we were, is and are; some would say gods and goddesses even.

So though I believe Black History Month plays an important role for those who aren't necessarily familiar with our culture, to me personally it's without a doubt more important to ensure Black history is taught in mainstream education in the correct way.

So, if say, all of a sudden Black history is taken up a notch in mainstream education would Black History Month still be relevant? Well as stated it has a role to play.

I believe a lot of effort is put into making the moment, season, effective and maybe that's where we go wrong. As effective shouldn't be the word I would want to find to describe Black History Month, it should be a moment where people are left in amazement, left with moments to remember.

Maybe there have been these moments, but for me personally, I can't really remember any significant moments in 30 years of Black History here in Leicester, but I am not complaining because as stated, I tend to view things from a different perspective.

I think here in Leicester Black History Month could be so much more significant. I think strategically we could work together much better as Black organisations. Today, for example, we seem to have pockets of people, organisations, working in isolation and I don't think this is the best way to deliver projects and events, where the aim is to empower our community. I would go even further by saying that Black History Month is more significant for every other community, culture of people. I think that Black History Month should be heavily promoted in predominantly 'white areas' and areas where there is a lack of people of our culture, people of African Heritage. I think exposing other peoples to our culture through a vehicle such as Black History Month would actually lead to greater cohesion between communities, through understanding, information, advice and guidance.

Have I been involved in any significant events, projects during past Black History Months? Yes I have, and have been for the last probably 20 years. Last year I worked a lot on promoting our Black Poppy Rose, whose objective is to promote the contributions of African Heritage people to the wars of the world. Another business project I promote heavily during Black History Month is our 'Freedom of Our Minds: Emancipation Walk'. We do this walk annually on the first Saturday of August.

Usually if I'm involved in Black History Month it's through my own events or promoting my events, though there have been occasions where I have attended events. Regarding the events I go to, they are usually centred on a 'Pan-African' ethos, having been organised by friends or are of particular significance.

So what sticks out for me in terms of memories when it comes to Black History Month? Not a lot to be honest, and that is the honest truth. Maybe it's the fact that I spent all of my teenage years growing up in the Caribbean and as such was never exposed to such a time of the year over there.

However as stated I'm a believer that Black History Month should be celebrated all year round as our history should be told from its 'past, present and future'.

So a bit of Black history for you; as you are aware my name is Freedom Tariq Zampaladus; my family name on my mother's side goes by the name of 'Wint'.

I had a great, great uncle who went by the name of 'Arthur Wint'; Arthur Wint was the first Jamaican athlete to win a gold medal at any Olympics way back in 1948 and I remind my three children about him constantly. So yes I have a strong bloodline connected to Black history and I believe passing such knowledge onto the next generation is just as significant as celebrating our achievements during a condensed month. Our children, like ourselves, are and have been constantly bombarded by negative images of Black culture. They need to be empowered frequently with positive images and messages in order to feed their creativity and make them feel good about themselves. So it should be incumbent on us to find positivity from within our own individual backgrounds or families to pass onto them. These images and messages do not necessarily have to be about great events or people. They could comprise positive stories about a grandmother, grandfather, uncle, aunt etc., who strived hard to accomplish something simple and good, who are held in high esteem and have great regard in our families.

Lastly it's extremely important that when we look into our history we ensure it is delivered by ourselves, has been approved by ourselves, and is honest to ourselves, giving our children something that is within their reach which can be grasped, thus empowering us and them rather than trying to embarrass us and them. In a nutshell it needs to come from an 'Afro-centric base rather than a Euro-centric base'.

"Black people have never had a history, it is what the colonial slave master did that was history. History is William Wilberforce and not the revolution in Haiti. African history is not Kwame Nkrumah and the Ghana movement and Tafawa Balewa and Nelson Mandela. It is how we, here in England, the whites, allowed Nelson Mandela through the gates. That's where history and the disfigurement of the history of Black people comes. That's why we are so revolutionary. That's why we fool so much. There's nothing. We come with a blank sheet. And all of history is what we were helped in doing, not what we did. What can I say to Black youth? I have seven children. So that's a direct speak to them, right? It's not Black youth in general. You have to know where you come from. Otherwise you don't know where you are going. You are led by a donkey by a rope from the neck. My slogan is all movement comes from self movement and not from external forces acting on the organism. That's how history represents itself in people, you know. Not in books, not in Black History Month. It's an attitude. History is a critical understanding of your past. Black History Month, what do I see? I am what I am because of what I have been."

Darcus Howe (2010)

CULTURAL PRACTITIONERS

Mellow Baku, performing as part of *Strange Fruit: A Tribute to Billie Holiday* for the launch of Black History Month 2015.

MELLOW BAKU

BLACK HISTORY MONTH GAVE ME A SAFE SPACE

My first encounter with Black History Month was through reconnection with my father Shango Baku, an actor, writer and Rasta-activist, who I met for the first time as a young adult. I was raised from age 5 in an autocratic commune that discouraged affiliation with any group, community or even family, except itself. When I left, I studied fine art in Leicester and discovered Black artists such as Lorna Simpson, Basquiat and Renee Stout, and was drawn to music I'd only heard in my earliest years: jazz, soul and reggae.

I began singing and recording in bands and performing jazz, but it was in my solo song writing and poetry that I began to share my personal and political voice. I've been fortunate to have this work commissioned and booked over the last 15 years as part of Black History Month celebrations and events.

I arrived in 'the world' of Leicester arts around 2000, having left a life that was largely disassociated with societal norms. This presented challenges for my understanding of the world around me, so that I often felt disconnected. As a person of mixed heritage born in the UK, I soon became aware of hierarchies, divisions and perceptions associated with 'Blackness', mixed-ness and race, perhaps more starkly given my background. At times I felt judged, lost or lacking without the framework, familiarity or vocabulary of ethnicity. Having little cultural understanding, it initially took me a while to even realise some of the work I was involved in was part of a Black History Month programme. But I came to value being included, as acknowledgement of both my art and my ancestry.

My first involvement was in the delivery of 12 weeks of sessions creating Anansi story-based art with children in a Brixton primary school. Since then, I've created spoken word performance in a three female line-up, led workshops and performed solo song, poetry and jazz. Most recently through commissions via Serendipity, I've diversified into script writing and narration for multimedia theatre piece *Paradigm Rhymes - Beyond the Dome*, and reinvented jazz song in *Strange Fruit: a Tribute to Billie Holiday* for the Black History Month Launch 2015. This year I perform my solo show *'Soon Come [...] Home'*, inspired by the poetry of Jean Binta Breeze.

Black History events enabled me, as an upcoming artist, to be included in the cultural context of the Black diaspora. To share my art, often a reflection of my exploration of Black identity, in a space that I found accepting, appreciative and rewarding.

Through performance opportunities I was able to connect with diverse artists, and have my voice recognised in the Black community. Commissions gave license to explore my Caribbean heritage. Furthermore, the breadth of what Black History Month represented assisted my journeys into jazz, afrobeat, and art of the wider Black diaspora. As my practice has progressed I've become more interested in how my art can facilitate awareness in people. Black History Month gives me a platform to develop aspects of this.

One might say that Black History Month has been a 'safe space' for my artistic exploration and expression. I hope this is true for many who have participated over the last three decades, whether as audience or creators.

67

In past Leicester events, the celebratory nature of an African Family day, or a drumming circle with Paulo Carnoth, has inspired kinship and belonging. In a programme of films, exhibitions or a performance or a workshop with Leicester/Jamaica's Jean Binta Breeze, affirmation could be found. An oration from much loved and now departed Griot, Wolde Selassie, provoked thought and challenged prejudice.

There have been many changes in Leicester over the last 15 years, with the arrival of new migrants. This is reflected in the groups of young people I lead Black History music workshops with 2 Funky Arts, City of Leicester College and other community organisations.

68

In an increasingly wider demographic mix of workshop participants, fewer children seem aware of the role of Black history in a western context and its influence in UK society. I often find many now demonstrate less understanding of what the blues sounds like, where it came from and how it influences music they hear today. I in turn hear other perspectives of African history, among the many cultures represented in a typical Leicester class. I enjoy the challenges this presents and the insights I gain from young people, but find it concerning that there appears to be less Black history presented in schools.

The emergence of diversity and intersectionality as concepts to facilitate equality in society, can be said to have benefitted many suffering the effects of marginalisation. Adopting these concepts have also contributed to the politicisation of identity.

This can lead to debate over what stories people can 'voice', who is allowed ownership or commentary on certain subjects, themes and expressions, depending on identity and heritage. And there is increasing debate around what Black History Month events should be, how they should be presented and by whom.

In light of the rise of anti-immigration sentiment and perceived racism in the UK over recent years, there's also an increasing call for more activism within cultural activities such as Black History Month.

Black history in the UK arose from Caribbean roots. From my first experiences this was evident; an open ease of approach, an overstanding of the importance of creative expression, passion for sharing stories that celebrate culture and achievement and always festivity; from the music, dance and the voices of the elders, to the rice and peas and dumpling.

Activism to me means challenging prejudice perceptions and conditioning through creative action. Having contributed to many other events that directly oppose prejudice. I've come to believe that activism within an inclusive, open approach has the best chance of transforming awareness. If Black History Month in the UK is to continue to deliver the kind of safe space for reflection I enjoyed, I believe future Black History Month will need to maintain or even widen its embrace to all that is Black, all who perceive themselves to be or wish to identify with Black.

The voices of those who initiated and continue to nurture its progress are still vital, enriched by new voices from the diaspora. Black History Month, from its roots to offshoots, can contribute powerfully to the growing voices that challenge bigotry and prejudice in the UK and globally. One Love.

Ili Sanchea, performing as part of *Strange Fruit: A Tribute to Billie Holiday* for the launch of Black History Month 2015.

Musician Fela Kuti performs at Orchestra Hall in Detroit, *Michigan (7 November 1986)*.
Photograph by Leni Sinclair/Michael Ochs Archives/Getty Images.

CULTURAL PRACTITIONERS

PAULO CARNOTH

BLACK HISTORY MONTH CHALLENGING ATTITUDES

My name is Paulo Carnoth. I am an Angolan and an African multi-disciplined artist, songwriter, poet, music producer, and African contemporary jewellery maker who has been resident in the UK since 2001. I hold a degree in Youth and Community Development awarded by De Montfort University in Leicester and am currently working as a support care worker for young people with autism.

I have been involved with Black History Month events ever since I came to the UK, participating in events mainly in Leicester, but also in many other cities. Through my work as a self-employed artist and workshop leader, delivering African arts in schools and hospitals, and at conferences and music events, I have been engaged with many organisations and projects that focus on the history and lives of Black people, and believe that Black History Month is still a valuable approach for informing, challenging attitudes and promoting diversity.

It is necessary with an event like Black History Month to ensure participants understand the purpose of the event. We need to explain to people, and especially the young, about the past and support them to achieve our common goal which is to live in a society where we are equal and the colour of skin no longer has any significance and where we do not have to struggle as victims of inequality, racism and discrimination.

There is more to share with people about African culture than dance, music, football or carnival. We should celebrate our arts with love and compassion so the new generation can understand and promote freedom and love. It is necessary to continue raising our voices, calling all African and African descendant artists, to embrace and celebrate their Black history. Throughout the Black History Month, we can spread the joy and the beauty of African arts and culture and use this as a vehicle that brings people together. We must encourage the Black communities to come together and share the values and the rich traditions that Africans have to offer. Black History Month should showcase our history and the traditional and contemporary aspects and values of our lives to allow other people to understand the way Africans and people of African descent live. Many people lost their lives for the liberation of the Black people so we must celebrate and remember the people that fought for our freedom from the colonial system. We mustn't forget the past, carved with blood, sweat and tears, but we must also move forward.

I believe it is time to bring the Black perspective into educational and academic institutions and the national curriculum so that students can learn more about the socio-cultural diversity of their country and build a society where every citizen is treated equally regardless of the colour of their eyes or their skin.

Black History Month projects still need on-going support and greater funding in order to deliver effective events. I also believe that Black people themselves need to take a greater lead in organising these events, as they most of all know their history and, more importantly, know how they want to shape their future.

DERRICK 'MR MOTIVATOR' EVANS

CARPE DIEM

I was listening to the radio yesterday, and callers phoned in with differing views about role models and how being Black was a disadvantage. They also expressed various mixed views on the need for Black History Month.

This got me thinking and I came to the realisation that all too often it is so easy to blame others for where we are and for what we do, not do or fail to achieve in life. Failure occurs because we fail to seize the opportunities that life offers us.

I am Jamaican by birth and I was given away at three months of age. In hindsight I would say that my mother made a good decision if you look at where I am now.

I do not recall having a definitive role model as I grew up, but rather driven by the desire to try everything as a means of becoming a success. At age seventeen I was living on my own in Leicester and my first role in life was to take responsibility for myself. I then became a single dad at the age of nineteen and my next role was to take responsibility for my daughter and provide for her. This was a difficult period of my life especially as all I had was the desire to be great. I had seen too many others who neglected the child that they had brought into the world.

I knew that I must be prepared to do whatever I had to do to ensure that I provided for her in the best way that I could. It was by no means easy but I did my best to make it work. We lived in a bed and breakfast, council flat, were homeless for a while, but I knew and believed that if I worked hard, eventually life would become better for us.

I couldn't afford much and propping the bed up with books was one of the only ways of keeping the rats off my sleeping daughter. But I still kept believing that good times would be not very far away. No one owed me anything, not government, society or any one individual, but I owed it to myself to pursue my goals diligently, with vigour and tenacity.

I had to learn how to plait her hair, then take her to the child-minder and pick her up at the end of the day on time. From there it was back home to feed her, bathe her and put her to bed, only to wake up the next day and start all over again.

I stacked shelves, I worked on a building site, I swept floors and cleaned toilets. Why? Because I had to take responsibility. But I never stopped believing that eventually with hard work and perseverance better times would come.

I was not a Black man struggling. I was simply a man fighting for survival. I was surrounded by prejudices and had to learn to rise above all that, but when I was asked at to my first job interview why had I not indicated on the phone that I was Black, I quickly retorted, "Well you didn't tell me you were white". To succeed in life you have to have a sense of humour as wearing a visible chip on your shoulder will only keep you back.

I am a man who has had to work and I learnt very early on that being Black is just another way of describing what I look like on the outside. I am faced with the same problems as everyone else and how I chose to overcome life's obstacles is to maybe just work a bit harder than most.

Black history is all around us everyday not just for the month, we are so blessed by Black people around us and equally we can learn so much from the successes

Mr Motivator

CULTURAL PRACTITIONERS

of others of any colour. There are so many successful individuals out there, and if they can do it then so can you. Everyone of us have the potential for greatness, you just have to want it more than others.

So to get ahead, you need an edge, something that makes you stand out from everyone else. Start with at least a basic education. Then you need to show a willingness to be the best at whatever we have to do. Initially, to get where we want to be, it may mean doing something that is not your thing because doing something is better than doing nothing. Doing something and doing it well is one of the best advertisements available to all of us. If you are being the best that you can be, they will see your potential, and who knows what they may offer you next.

So in life surprise yourself with how much you can do and strive to go beyond what is expected. Don't ever give up hope as all good things come to those who wait.

You must stop wearing a chip on your shoulder and strive for excellence in all things. Bob Marley spoke of mental slavery but what did he mean? For too long we go on about the past rather than focusing on the future, we talk about role models when we don't have to look far to see so many great individuals who pursued a dream, had a gem of an idea and made it happen.

Think of the fabulous chefs, all the great runners, tennis players, basketball players, music industry moguls, film actors, cricketers, corner shop proprietors, millionaires and billionaires. The role models are there for everyone to see, all you have to do this Black History Month is open your eyes and your minds.

You can choose to follow them and be inspired by them. Instead of just dreaming, .you can wake up and make it happen. Let's be honest, it wont be overnight, it will not happen immediately, but if you are determined and focused you will make it happen.

The price of success is perseverance. You cannot stop being Black, that is with you forever. Be proud of your heritage, be happy with who you are, and armed with all the ammunition life gave you, get up and be who you want to be.

Just ask yourself, "Are you ready to be great?" If you are, open your arms and embrace it.

74

PHILIP HERBERT

BLACK CLASSICAL MUSIC NEEDS A PLACE ON THE CALENDAR

Black History Month is a time and place on the calendar where the opportunity for exploring creative, historic and enlightening narratives is given to the Black creative community at large to be able to discover new perspectives of peoples across the African diaspora who are often prejudged, or ignored when considering their creative output.

As a composer and educator, it is equally exciting to be able to explore and research project ideas, which come from the depths of Black history. The process of conveying my ideas comes through music that is constructed by using classical music as the vehicle for revelations of new creative perspectives of Black historical heritage. I have an eclectic interest in music of all kinds, that comes from the African diaspora. It is through melding some of these musical strands in classical form that breathes new life into the a newly created composition, whose expression is to enhance and amplify perspectives that give new insights into Black history and the experience of Black historical context.

I recall the journey through the London 2012 Project, 'Ballare: To Dance', where my *Suite for Solo Steel Pan and Strings'*, as an original idea and concept challenged and smashed the stereotypes of roles played by musical instruments. This for me is a key perspective to share with audiences made up of people from a diverse cross section of the community in the United Kingdom. Instead the classical musical instruments (strings) in the suite, accompanied the solo steel pan, as opposed to taking the lead. The world musical instruments (the Guitar, the Sitar, the Bandoneon, the Solo Steel Pan) took the lead in

various scores or in a piece from Cuba; the string players were challenged by the composer, Guido Lopez Gavilan, to play their instruments like percussion instruments. There was also the role that Lee Payne played as a tap dancer, using his feet as a percussionist would, as an extension of the percussion section in the orchestral ensemble. From an educational perspective, this project took a musical journey around the world across the African diaspora, India, Cuba, Mexico, Argentina, and Spain, and although the musical sound worlds from these countries were evident aurally, the fact that world music instruments sat side by side with classical musical instruments on stage, whilst some musicians from a classical training background read musical scores and others from a world music background relied on aural memory; the reality was that everyone was able to work together successfully, much to the relief of the audiences who attended the performances. In a microcosm, human beings of different backgrounds should be able to work together, sharing different perspectives but working towards one common goal. These are important and valuable lessons to convey as a composer and as an educator. The support for this project by Serendipity was invaluable in nurturing the creative process right up until the premiere in Leicester. The project also enjoyed wider public access via an interview that I gave for BBC Radio 3's In Tune with Suzy Klein, where one movement from the Suite for Solo Steel Pan and Strings was performed live just after the interview.

Black History Month has also provided me with a very valuable opportunity to showcase projects such as 'Lost Chords, Unsung Songs', where chamber music and art

Philip Herbert *(26 August 2015)*. Photographer Mike Sewell, Leicester Mercury.

songs from the Harlem Renaissance were performed in a concert programme. This recital programme provided an opportunity to explore the creative ideology that inspired composers, artists, poets, and creative individuals from a variety of backgrounds, of the Harlem Renaissance who looked back at African civilisations to see what had been achieved, to inspire new works within the Harlem Renaissance. This too is an important inspirational link with the past and present when surveying the voyage of Black creativity across previous timelines in different centuries. It was interesting that this concert programme provoked many questions about how and why this repertoire came to be created.

It was important that this project was supported by Serendipity in Leicester and also enjoyed a wider tour, where it reached Birmingham's CBSO Centre, as a project that was selected for the finals of the National Decibel showcase. In addition, an interview was given for BBC Radio 3's In Tune, to outline the tour of this project ending in the Purcell room at the Southbank Centre and to talk about the origins of the music and the composers who had created the music. The PR created for this event was read by a producer who had an idea for a BBC Radio 4 programme, which was to be presented by the Jazz Composer and Pianist, Julian Joseph, and entitled 'The Trumpet shall sound', for which I was invited to be a contributing expert.

77

History teaches that creative people of African origin dispersed their creative energies around the world and that for some reason some of this musical activity has been forgotten and as a result become hidden. I consider my role to facilitate the promotion of these hidden works as a matter of importance to preserve Black classical music heritage, as well as creating new work that can be heard during Black History Month or at a different point in the year. Without Black History Month, it is very easy to lose sight of the work of celebrated composers such as William Grant Still, Florence Price, George Walker, Le Chevalier de Saint Georges, Margaret Bonds, José Mauricio Nunes Garcia and many more. This work is important from an educational point of view, so that future generations of young Black people can learn about their cultural heritage, to give them a strong sense of cultural identity, to act as ambassadors and catalysts for future creative endeavours in the lineage of Black musical history.

Lee Payne, who performed as part of *Ballare: To Dance (2012).* Performing here at The Bell in Ticehurst.

LOUISE KATEREGA

NOT JUST ONE MOMENT, NOT JUST ONE MONTH... BLACK HISTORY MONTH FOR LIFE

For me, Leicester's Black History Month and my own history as a person of colour are inexorably intertwined. Leicester itself, and Black History Month in particular, I now realise as I look back are when my own Black history truly began and continues to this day.

The two works I was involved in making and performing for it back in 1999 have gone on to be a profound part of my own professional story, leading me directly onto all sorts of platforms and opportunities around the UK and beyond. More profoundly though, they led me to deep and lasting friend and colleague-ships with the others involved in them. Black History Month 1999 was literally the making of me inside and out. My small moments in the roll call of Leicester's Black History Month were not just something that happened to me, not just something I did, they helped me become who I am, as an artist, as a human being and a proud adopted daughter of the city.

I describe myself as mixed or dual heritage – Black Ugandan father, White English mother. Do I feel more Black or White? Both. And it's a gift. And it's a journey....

By the time, I arrived in Leicester in 1996, not long graduated from Warwick University (BA Hons. Film and Literature) and still with one foot in the West Midlands running a small contemporary dance company, I had barely encountered even my own Black history.

My parents separated before my birth and though they remained on extraordinarily good terms, I wrote to my Dad regularly and saw him yearly until age 14, he spoke little of our Ugandan cultural heritage. Born in 1969, my mother raised me in North Wales. In twenty years there, I encountered three other Black children across a school career.

The first other young Black people I encountered were my peers in the first ever National Youth Dance Company – from Leicester, Leeds and all second-generation Caribbean. I could trace my roots straight back to Africa. I couldn't slide in and out of patois. We connected through dance, but I could not connect culturally.

Like many of my generation my Black history touchstones were American, particularly 'Roots' when I was seven, which tangential though it was to my daily experience, was deeply affecting in terms of raising my self-worth. I too had a story. I too could be a storyteller through writing and performance.

Then it was a long wait 'til 'The Color Purple' by Alice Walker in American literature at university. This time the reaction was a little angrier: how come you had to get to a rarefied corner of higher education to see yourself reflected as a Black female writer or character in 'great literature'?

I owe that book a lot (not least that common love of it got me talking to my now best friend) and that was probably the beginning of a consciousness which by the time I was invited to participate in my first Leicester Black History Month in 1999 was ripe for development.

The two works in question are 'DNA: Destiny's Natural Ally', a solo, well a duet for a dancer and a rope, choreographed on me by of the finest natural daughter of the city, Sheron Wray, now Professor Sheron Wray PhD in the States, and back then hugely successful ex member of London Contemporary Dance Theatre and choreographer of her own outfit JazzExchange.

79

Louise Katerega in *DNA: Destiny's Natural Ally.*
Photographer Sally Hossack.

CULTURAL PRACTITIONERS

The second work which appeared on the same bill was one of my first professional choreographic attempts 'Between The Stones and The Stars', a quartet for two men and two women, one Black, one White in each pair, set to a collaboration between English and South African choral singers.

The title of the evening was 'Griotgraphies' (combining 'griot' as in Afrikan oral history and choreography as in dance making) as up until that point there had been few dance contributions to Black History Month in Leicester. The bill was completed by a third piece, a duet by Leicester-born Kwesi Johnson.

It was performed in the main gallery of New Walk Museum, back then quite an unusual move. Apart from the obvious link to the notion of history and that it is one of the most beautiful atmospheric, performance spaces in Leicester, the museum was also chosen as a Black reclamation of a very Victorian space with its obvious connotations of slavery and white cultural dominance.

'Griotgraphies' was bigger than just this evening, in that it ran alongside an exhibition of African artefacts unearthed from New Walk's vaults and curated by local scholar/griot/poet Wolde Selassie.

Part of our commission as choreographers/performers was to have some engagement with Wolde and the theme of the exhibition which was essentially to remind the world that the history 'Africa' has given the world is not just artistic and traditional, it is scientific and forward thinking. Indeed to truly know Afrikan history, not just the 'white' version of it, is to know that art, science, ritual and quest are all part of the same cultural

practice. Egypt, moreover, in this 'white' version has been cut off from sub-Saharan Africa to be seen as a separated more sophisticated entity. Our job was to re-claim and claim anew the place of early Black science only just being discovered to pre-date much thought to have developed in Europe.

There is no other expression for this than to say, the above facts and the research it encouraged us all to consider, blew my maturing mind! Wolde pointed me at books I had never heard were genres let alone titles, I looked at Egypt with an enthusiasm I have never previously experienced, I came to understand the history, the geography, astronomy, anthropology I had taken for granted in an entirely new way.

For the ins and outs of this, I refer you to the works themselves and their programme notes. The story I want to finish up here is the one about what Black History Month 1999 led me to next.

Because of the portability and economy (only one dancer to rehearse, only one to pay!) of a solo like DNA, I have been able to share it several times again.

The Phoenix Arts Centre (now Sue Townsend Theatre) was instrumental in building my relationships with programmers Judi Hughes and Matthew Linley.

Matthew was a key early programmer of my company Foot in Hand founded in 2003. (One of my Griotgraphies dancers, Beverley Voice was also its first secretary. Matthew eventually became Foot in Hand's Chair after supporting my entry into the prestigious Bloomberg Place Prize for choreography

81

with a piece that made history as the first to feature disabled dancers at professional level. Those dancers moreover went on to serve Leicester in shows and ceremonies linked to the 2009 Special Olympics and 2012 Paralympics.

A year after DNA, I went to South Africa on the first four trips in three years, courtesy of the British Council. On my last 2003 trip, I performed DNA at FNB Dance Umbrella in Johannesburg, the country's premiere dance festival after warming it up at Britain's Resolution! Festival at The Place. Best performances, responses and reviews I have ever had. Sheron and I spoke recently and fondly of it as both of our favourite, most satisfying work (to date!).

In South Africa, I finally experienced being instantly spotted as African and as mixed and finally experienced life within a number of Black cultures not just being Black. Applying this to my UK situation, I took a new view of myself and embraced Carol Leeming's invitation to become a member of Leicester African Caribbean Arts Forum, contributors at the time to Black History Month, not just because I was Black, but because I am British and Caribbean people are a huge influence on the place I call home. And Leicester was my home. The education begun by 'Griotgraphies' was complete.

'Between The Stones and The Stars' was revived and re-worked in 2006 for Mission Re-Position, State of Emergency's national tour by Black British female choreographers. I thoroughly enjoyed the re-visit and being able to refer to the original work on video saved time and pressure on both myself and the dancers.

Special Olympics 2009 Opening Ceremony with *'One-derland'* carnival costumes by Mahogany Arts.
Photographer Ian Davis, reproduced with permission of Leicester City Council.

I have just in fact helped one of those dancers get a visa to work in America with a reference about her work on that 'Between The Stones 2.0' so it continues to have a profound effect on another mixed heritage female dancer's career.

Though the pieces diverged over time, yet there is one person who links them and remains linked to me. Now Manchester based Joanne Bernard, ex-Kokuma, founding member of ACE Dance Music danced in the original 'Between The Stones' and so brought both insight and freshness to it as rehearsal director on the Re-Position Tour of 2006. She danced in the Place Prize and in 2009 she joined Foot in Hand for an eight-month project performing in one piece and rehearsal directing the other playing and 'power sharing' both roles with me in a spirit of trust I am not sure I will ever know again. I also had the privilege of touring with her and fellow 'Between The Stones' dancer Stewart Thomas (also of Leicester) for State of Emergency in 2005, on which they did finally teach me patois, but that's a whole other story...

Afterthought

As I have been writing this it's a story I realise that I have barely ever articulated even to myself. As in 1999, Black History Month has been once again calling me to express an important but as yet unexpressed part of me. It has been a privilege to share it in this way.

We are questioning whether Black History Month should still exist as a separate entity: Is it a ghetto? An echo-chamber? A cul-de-sac? Should Black history not be happening everywhere and all year round nowadays? Does it even need that distinctive name?

I look back at my own history, which exists because of it, my answers are as follows; without that welcoming in, without that safe space, without that valuing of the Black part of myself I was offered as a young artist I would not have grown the wings I grew to take that work and what I learned from it to many other contexts, to many other people who are not Black or who think Black people are not their concern. For me, so long as at least some people are using special interest spaces as a through route back into the outside world, a corridor not a cul-de-sac, a recording for pod-cast not an echo-chamber that all works for me. Some can choose to keep things porous for those who do not want to, nor should ever be forced to, mix very much or even at all outside those special interest groups. They are the specialists, we who seek to spread their knowledge to others, need them to focus.

Yes, absolutely Black history should be happening everywhere and always too. Well having just enjoyed David Olusogas's wonderful 'Black British History' series on BBC we see that it is and always has been. Our task is now to keep pushing the general Western populace via many means not just tucked away documentaries to recognise it! Turn and keep pushing the gatekeepers to turn, a few more of the incredible stories Black history yields it holds into widely-shown, compelling artworks to catch more and more of that public's attention.

Does it need to be Black? Well it did for me. If nothing else my story shows Black people, even or perhaps especially those of us who are not all Black, need Black history too. Black History Month reconnected me with a lost part of myself I was never going get reconnected to via any other means. My well-intentioned white parent and community couldn't do it (couldn't find the writings, didn't know where to look). The school system didn't. It still doesn't do nearly the job it could. Film and broadcasting ditto. Though at least we finally see some consciousness of that in terms of the latter and bring on the action.

The internet is a profound opportunity. Wish I'd had what we have now when I was researching my dances back in 99! However, we still need to exercise choice in our use of it and as we know it's already hip to that and happy to help us set up information echo-chambers of our own clicking!

So where else then apart from Black History Month can we still access the space to learn and grow like I did? Things are so much better but I am not confident all its functions have been replaced yet...

I hope my story shows that one Black History Month in one person's life can have long-lasting effects on that person and that person's input to the world far beyond that last a lifetime. I had one cultural moment which cultivated a oneness in me absolutely necessary for me to join in and foster an ambition to join up - the rest of the world.

85

Soweto Kinch performing Nonagram at the launch of *Black History Month (2016)*. Photographer Matt Cawrey.

86

Duncan's father, *Lloyd Earl 'Larry' Lawrence.* The portrait was submitted for British national photography award in the early 1960's. Photographer Alfred Ferguson.

DUNCAN LAWRENCE

GROWING ROOTS

My father was an officer in the Royal Air force and it was difficult to establish deep roots in any particular community due to him being posted or promoted to different parts of the country. As a teenager I remember going with my auntie to a local market stall in East London and buying a T-Shirt with the words of Marcus Garvey (cited in Bogues, 2003);

> *"A people without the knowledge of their past history, origin and culture is like a tree without roots."*

I wore that shirt with such pride and kept the words in my head to help me face the reality of being one of three Black boys in the school, one of which was my older brother! Links to my heritage were further forged through regular visits to family in London and Bristol as well as regularly attending the Notting Hill Carnival during the 1980s.

Arriving In Leicester – what an adventure...

In 2001 I was called to make a spiritual journey from West to East, Midlands that is, some 47 miles. Along with my wife I led a mission team, set up to support Christians from our mother church in Birmingham who were living in Leicester and found the commute increasingly difficult. In that year we formed the Leicester Church of Christ, a Christian fellowship in the heart of multicultural Leicester, based at the YMCA East Street.

Before moving lock, stock and barrel to Leicester we decided to pay a visit to get a flavour of what it had to offer. We had heard the word multicultural bandied about and were expecting to be immersed in an African, Caribbean and Indian melting pot. But it didn't quite meet up to that expectation as we ambled down Granby Street into the heart of the city.

It took us a while to settle in when we finally made the move, and we relied heavily on the emotional and spiritual support of our church family. The timing of Black history proved to be important for me as a minister because as part of the church services on Remembrance Sunday I felt it was important to ensure that our congregation remembered men and women from the Commonwealth who had served during the World Wars.

I had learnt from events during the October Black History Month about Black men and women and their impact on British culture. So the Black History Month was a necessary point in the calendar where resources, articles and media became more readily available and I was able to seize the chance to glean information for inspirational facts.

It was at the YMCA that I had the good fortune to meet Wolde Selassie. My wife, who was the main Sunday school teacher invited him and his African drumming school to be part of the Sunday school class. The kids loved him and his teachings on Africa and African drumming!

Where had all the Black people gone?

In the early noughties, my third year living in Leicester, I remember my wife and I being invited by our then neighbours to an event at the Phoenix Arts Centre on Upper Brown Street, Leicester. The play, Love and Marriage and New York City by David Heron, was part of Black History Month and was termed a Black romantic comedy. Upon arriving early, we seized the front row seats. My wife and I were excited to be with our new neighbours in a beautiful dimly lit theatre. The play was a blast but to our amazement when the lights came up we turned around and saw the hall - nuff Black people!! We thought where did all you guys come from! Most of whom we had never seen before! Needless to say we stopped a while to chat!

Our reaction was reflective of how we were still trying to get to know our African and Caribbean community whilst still finding our social feet in Leicester. So for us in the early years of our arrival to Leicester, the Black History Month programme created a forum and platform enabling us to meet peers and members of our community.

The value of Black History Month

Regarding the educational value of Black History Month, I agree that it ought to have a high profile for a 4 or 5-week period in the month celebrating Black history in Leicester. I don't think it can be sustained throughout the year with the same intensity but I do believe there *should* be an on-going programme of educating events in Leicester and across the UK that keeps Black culture in the public eye. I believe the main focus should be through schooling, mentorships and positive Black role models that children can see, hear and most importantly interact with. From my experiences Black History Month has an important role in Leicester to connect people to their cultural roots, re-educate all peoples about Black history, the history that in a lot of cases has been supressed and not allowed to be told. It also needs to showcase the many areas that African, Caribbean and Black British culture has excelled in across the arts, sciences and business.

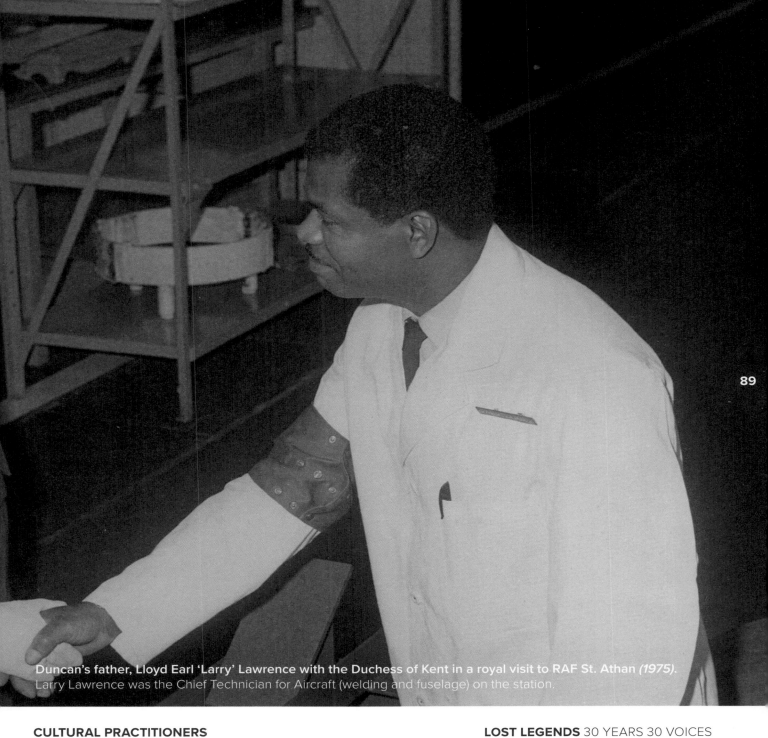

Duncan's father, Lloyd Earl 'Larry' Lawrence with the Duchess of Kent in a royal visit to RAF St. Athan *(1975)*.
Larry Lawrence was the Chief Technician for Aircraft (welding and fuselage) on the station.

Carol Leeming *(7 March 1988).* Photographer Ming de Nasty.

CAROL LEEMING

BLACK HISTORY/HERSTORY

My own father helped to instil in me a strong sense of Black identity, pride and achievement, with a desire for knowledge from an early age, as well as highlighting the effects of pernicious racism. I have always been strongly committed to my own continued learning and promoting of Black history/herstory in Leicester. Over many years this has been in various roles as volunteer, advocate, manager, producer, curator, mentor, director and artist.

In the 1980s in Leicester, I had read numerous Black books, that were only available from Raddle Books Leicester. It was a pivotal exciting time; my community involvement included African Caribbean Education Group, Saturday School for African Caribbean Children, then held at Moat Community College in Leicester. Working alongside as volunteers, with members of the Black Sister's Group, including Nelista Cuffy, a teacher, and Donna Jackman, a community development worker/activist. Along with others, we committed ourselves, to disseminating Black history/herstory and culture, firstly across the African Caribbean diaspora communities and more widely to other communities in Leicester/shire.

Our rationale was best exemplified in a later statement made by local community activist Perse Thomas to paraphrase *Black history, is my history, your history, is our history*. Black history therefore starts from before Roman times in the UK, from Ancient Kemet/Eygpt to the very present, including more recent shared legacies, of the slave trade - an African holocaust, and the effects of both imperialism and colonialism.

I and my Black women colleagues, thereby were fulfilling our individual and collective roles, as conscious Black Women supporting our community, providing much needed strong Black feminist/womanist, Afrocentric perspectives politically, with regard to Black history/herstory, as members of both Leicester Black Sisters Group and the fledgling African Education Group. Meanwhile, the African Caribbean Saturday School, importantly, was teaching Black history/herstory to African Caribbean children, alongside the teaching of basic school subjects such as mathematics and English.

This Leicester African Caribbean Saturday School work was ably supported, crucially with Black history, books, visual materials for display and games, such as Nubian Jak, which taught Black history. These resources were available from Raddle Books on Melbourne Road Highfields area of Leicester.

In particular, the support and initiation of a specific annual Black History Month in London during the month of October by the Greater London Council, spurred us in Leicester to quickly follow, as it did in many other cities, to organise our own Black History events, spearheaded by Raddle Books and specifically Wolde Selassie. Black History Months across the UK were established, with *grassroots African Caribbean groups, organisations and individuals taking the lead*.

In Leicester, Raddle Books, the Highfields Workshop/Imani Ujimaa Centre, now the African Caribbean Centre, alongside Ajani Women and Girls Centre, were part of this new development. However, the Ajani Centre actively promoted Black history/herstory throughout the year, with all types of activities including arts and cultural, visual materials, books and events, workshops, speakers, with Kwaanza events, and visits to see famous Black women writer events and performing artists.

In time, links forged with Raddle Books, Highfields Workshop and Ajani Centre, led them all to collectively and individually host Black History Month community events during October annually for a month. The impetus, knowledge, information and resources, were mainly coming from Raddle Books and its contacts and among Black women in Ajani Centre, who travelled and made links nationally with other Black women groups and organisations.

In particular, Wolde Selassie, as mentored by Elder Brother Koko from South Africa, with regard to African diaspora historical, cultural knowledge and cultural practices, led to this important knowledge being shared over a period of time with myself and many others in our community. Wolde's personal contribution, therefore, was particularly invaluable to me personally, to other Ajani Centre founder members and the wider community, both the African Caribbean diaspora community, and the statutory and voluntary organisations along with the wider community of Leicester and Leicestershire.

In time it was agreed to try to coordinate all the events and activities, offered by the African Caribbean community, statutory and voluntary sector organisations for the Black History Month. Wolde Selassie was very involved in this early development. A significant highlight was the *Griotgraphies* launch event and exhibition curated by Wolde Selassie. The launch event included an outdoor promenade, with assorted drummers and percussionists, which led launch attendees down to the museum, with choir music performance and myself as Griot Story teller and soloist with Kainé Choir.

Later in 1999 it was decided to coordinate with a small budget provided by Leicester City Council, for the Leicester Black History Season launch event and brochure, with the Leicester Black History Consortium to lead and oversee the programme. My further involvement in Leicester Black History Month continued as arts manager of the re-organised Leicester Caribbean Arts Forum (LACAF) that took over successfully leading and coordinating the Leicester Black History Season, the BHS Consortium and its launch events.

In one year, *Africa* was the theme set, a specific highlight included a successful Haymarket series of events over three nights, titled *Nubian Star Lounge*. It featured commissioned LACAF artists that I had mentored to produce new work for their first time. It was produced, directed and marketed by me as arts manager at LACAF, the programme included drama, dance, music and poetry.

Other successful LACAF events which I led as arts manager and curated that garnered both good local media coverage and large audiences, was the LACAF annual *African Family Day* held at Moat Community College. It offered Afrocentric activities, for all ages, such as a Community African Libation, speakers on Afrocentric topics, African Caribbean social history (with the late Roi Kwabena), folk storytellers, African Caribbean games, craft workshops, with beading, braiding, tie dye and batik, performance, African Caribbean drumming and dance, and

92

African Caribbean food. The Black History Season grew into a two-month season over October and November, reflecting the levels of participation of different individuals, groups, organisations, and individuals, across the wider community of Leicester and Leicestershire.

LACAF undertook to better promote more education and understanding, and better overall coordination of activities, for Black History Season.

To this end, a theme was set by Leicester BHS Consortium, as follows, *Black History, is my history, is your, is our history*, as provided by Perse Thomas, to help facilitate appropriate wider engagement in the programme of Black History Season.

Later on, for a brief time, the Leicester Black History Season was coordinated and led by myself working also as creative manager at Mainstream Partnership (a regional BME Arts organisation) along with the Black History Consortium. It was agreed to use the above statement as the overarching theme, with sub themes to be set by Black History Consortium annually. Overseeing audience development and marketing was also part of my role for the season.

Another key highlight and proud moment for me was my role as co-curator and art director for my company, Dare to Diva, and LACAF, in partnership with Leicester Museum; we produce *Style Up*, an accompanying launch event and local Black fashion exhibition, alongside a prestigious touring V&A Exhibition on the history of Black style and fashion. This work included two part photographic local exhibitions: of the Leicester African Caribbean community sourced archives and of photographs and fashion artefacts from the 1950s to the present, documenting local African Caribbean style and fashion across the generations.

As part of the *Style Up* project, I also recruited and trained young Black people as models, atavistically styled in an Afrocentric fashion, by me as art director and stylist for a photographic shoot for a second photographic exhibition. This historical event also featured a fashion show with Afrocentric contemporary clothes by a local African designer. The event also offered African Caribbean food and drink sponsored by Guinness. It was a spectacular, well attended event, with big numbers later viewing the exhibitions over the forthcoming weeks.

I later chaired and led the Black History Season Consortium, as coordinated by Mainstream Partnership, providing an introduction to the season's brochure, highlighting the important Afrocentric themes. A particular joy and highlight was the very successful BHS Launch and additional launch of an exhibition about Mary Seacole at Leicester New Walk Museum. The event also had a speaker on the fundraising campaign, for a statue of Mary Seacole, which has now been successful, with the statue erected in London.

My more recent roles within Leicester Black History Month, as led by Pawlet Brookes, Serendipity include being an assessor of Black artists that have applied for a Serendipity led, Arts Council funded commissioned opportunity *BHM Live*, to produce and showcase new arts work. I have also been a music artist performing some of Billie Holiday's repertoire, at the centenary celebration of her life *Strange Fruit: a Tribute to Billie Holiday* in 2015. This stunning, well attended, flagship event was commissioned and delivered by Serendipity at City Hall Leicester.

MADU MESSENGER

SHARED RELATIONSHIP

I've always had an interest in history, the stories of the world's nations and peoples; but it's the history of Black people in this country, that I have a particular passion for.

I remember going on a school trip to New Walk Museum, I don't know if it is still there, but there was a big oil painting of a Georgian scene. As I looked, I noticed that what I thought was the edge of the curtain, was in fact a Black servant holding a drinks tray. He was barely visible, tucked away in the *'blackground'* as I call it.

For me at that young age it made quite an impression; it was my first indication that Black people have been here in Britain for quite some time, and not just since the arrival of my parent's generation. Nowadays there is a lot more recognised evidence of a Black presence in this country going back thousands of years.

I remember in the past Black History Month focused a lot on the historical greatness of Africa and was quite African-American in its content. But I was always more interested in the lives of Black peoples, even if they were only a small percentage of the population that lived in this country. I have always viewed their stories more applicable to our situation; being born in Britain and facing similar social struggles to what they would have experienced just because they were seen as other.

I see educating not only ourselves but also the wider public on Black history in this country as very important, because whether we like it or not, our histories are intertwined. We are here because we are all products of the British Empire and our input and contribution in turn has helped to socially shape and construct the country.

We were there when Catherine of Aragon, wife of Henry VIII, travelled to London with her African attendants. During the seventeenth and eighteenth centuries an estimated 20,000 Black people were living just in London alone with other communities in cities like Cardiff and Liverpool. Black sailors were there with Nelson at the Battle of Trafalgar and black soldiers served throughout the Napoleonic campaigns.

Many of the nation's stately homes that we see were built from the proceeds of slavery and it has also to be argued that it was the wealth generated from Britain's sugar industry and cotton trade, via its colonies in the Americas, that was the catalyst that helped to kick start its industrial revolution. The wealth that was acquired made possible the invention and entrepreneurship that lay the foundations of our modern world.

During both World Wars our forefathers from the Caribbean and the peoples of Britain's other dominions, answered the call of the Mother country and volunteered to do their duty. And when they were invited to help rebuild Britain after WWII they again came to work in the hospitals, transport and the building trades. In the face of overt racist attacks, covert racism within the job place and discrimination when trying to find accommodation where they were met with signs saying 'No Irish, No Blacks, No Pets', our foreparents endured. Despite these factors we as a people continue to survive and move forward with a small few even managing to reach the echelons of the nation's political system.

94

And even though they can be seen as stereotypical outlets, within the realms of sports, arts, music and entertainment, Black people have excelled.

From our urban centres, as in the past, each successive generation has developed its own musical statement that has reflected its experience within the societies that they live: dub reggae, hip-hop, jungle, drum and bass, grime, dub-step. These are genres of music that, like blues and jazz before them, have ended up being adopted by the wider populous. All of this is part of our history, our legacy in these modern times, a history that can help to give a sense of who we were, who we are, and who we may become.

To me, this is why Black History Month is an important event because it serves a dual purpose, firstly as a means by which we, as a people, can empower ourselves, and secondly as a medium by which the wider demographic of society can view our historical presence and contribution.

Having been to university to study the immigration history of both Britain and the US and knowing aspects of history in general, there is also another reason why I believe Black History Month is important. It is important because it can be used as a means to educate and spread the wider knowledge of the historical presence and contributions of Black people in the West. A vehicle by which the present growth in xenophobic tendencies can be countered. After all, knowledge can affect change.

I remember quite by accident I was watching something on the television, about a woman from Birmingham who was slightly bigoted, due to her let's say white privilege. It turns out an ancestor of hers had moved from the Caribbean to Britain sometime in the late 1800s. Her journey of discovery took her back to the West Indies and the family home of her ancestor. Funny thing was, as I watched, I recognised the house! It was my grandfather's house and my uncle, whom I'd not seen since I was young, was there showing the woman a picture of his father, my grandfather, the same picture that I have sitting on my mantelpiece. In this instance, for her, knowledge affected a change that hopefully made her a little more conscious.

This personal anecdote serves to illustrate just how much all of our histories are intertwined whether we know it or not, or whether we accept it or not. The role of Black History Month serves not only as a means of empowering people of the African diaspora, it also reflects our historical and continued shared relationships within the societies that we live.

66We should have long ago put to bed the myth that there is any history of Britain that does not include the stories of the darker peoples from the colonies. Truly decolonising the curriculum would entail deconstructing the Eurocentric basis for our study of history. Tinkering at the edges will not solve this crisis of knowledge.**99**

Kehinde Andrews (2017)

96

Racist graffiti on a house occupied by two Nigerian men in Belfast *(19 August 2013).*
Photographer Stephen Barnes/Alamy Live News

Quincy

QUINCY

LEGACY AND PRIVILEGE

My name is Quincy; I have been a stand up comedian for over 10 years. What does Black History Month mean to me?

Well, I will tell you as you asked the question.

My journey starts in Africa; my parents are from the Caribbean island of Barbados who both came to the UK for different reasons. My mum was a nurse and my dad was in the army. They decided to get married, have me and two others came after. We were born in the heart of the East End, where I spent in the playground playing the most of my days. (Sorry, couldn't resist.)

Not only is that a lot of air miles and loyalty points but this path has stories to tell. What I'm trying to say here is that I have a lot to say about Black History Month from my point of view; I think my journey via various parts of the world is quite interesting. This has moulded me into the person I am today and I would say I have drawn on my history for comedic material.

As a comedian, Black History Month is probably the only time we get to perform on a regular basis around the country. At first, I used to look at the month of October as a time to make that money and stock up on the presents for Christmas. Now as a mature and wiser comedian, it's a month to use this as an opportunity to deliver knowledge, facts and relay stories with a comical twist. Having the ability to make people laugh is a gift, but to add education to make people think at the same time is a bonus in my book.

I tend to pick and choose which shows I do now as it's about quality instead of quantity. We live in an age that information can come in all forms or disguises.

It can be read and interpreted wrongly sometimes. It can be regurgitated most of the time. But a comedian will always stand out when the delivery is from the heart and delivered with passion. This is what I pride my performance on at all times but even more so for Black History Month.

As I sit here with my fingers on the keypad, I say to myself, apart from stating the obvious -

"What does Black History Month mean to me?"

It means legacy and being privileged to be a part of a race, who have come so far in the Western world and still found success.

To be able to share the history of great individuals who have helped build the UK and like any great inventor, being recognised for it, so they can smile down upon us from the start.

As much as it's important to acknowledge our ancestors of the past, it is our duty to empower our brothers and sisters of the future, so they continue the works of those before them.

For Black History Month, it isn't just about the Black community teaching our own. It's about teaching and showing people of different backgrounds how beautiful our culture is and how much we can learn from each other.

I will always remember my father telling me this as a young boy, and I have told this to my own children:

Even though the Black community make up only 8 to 10% of the UK, "big wheels cannot function without small cogs".

This to me, is what Black History Month stands for.

VICTOR RICHARDS

STREETS PAVED WITH GOLD

First of all, I would like to express my gratitude for the opportunity to celebrate the thirtieth anniversary of Black History Month in Leicester. As a playwright, poet and storyteller specialising in Windrush one man plays, my involvement in Black History Month is an inextricable part of my life. There are so many treasured memories of Black History Month in Leicester, as well as many cities across the UK.

In 1996 I produced my first play 'Streets Paved with Gold' through the Next Stage Diploma course at the Sandfield College in Nottingham where I studied drama. Geoff Bullen, who was the course director of productions and the diploma course (now associate director of the Royal Academy of Dramatic Art in London) inspired my dreams in believing that I could do this historic Windrush one man play – not just well, but successfully. Tony Graves who was then the African arts producer at the Nottingham Playhouse (now Principal Lecturer Arts Management at De Montfort University) gave me a break to perform my play and this was my first professional work in Black History Month.

One of my most memorable moments of Black History Month in Leicester is my major theatre performance of my play 'Streets Paved with Gold' at the old Haymarket Theatre in 1998. At that time, not many Black artists had the chance to perform at the Leicester's Haymarket Theatre. One day I courageously walked in the theatre, auditioned my play and was given the opportunity to perform at the theatre. It was a full house two-nights successful run. This experience gave me the confidence and helped me to launch my tour nationally and internationally. 1998 was the year marked as the

fiftieth anniversary of the arrival of the Empire Windrush. I was so excited to take part in the celebration and was very proud of my contribution to our community.

It's a wonderful experience when you discover the art of communication with people on a variety of occasions. I have visited so many Caribbean Elders Day centres to perform my play for our elders across the country including the Caribbean Court here in Leicester. My performances stimulated their minds and memories and it was fantastic to see their positive reactions.

As my work is specialising in theatre in education, I've had numerous opportunities to work with schools across the UK, especially schools who need to do something for children in Black History Month, many schools have said my work ticks all the boxes in their national curriculum as my plays and workshops cover British history, racism and cultural diversity.

Over the years, I have performed, taught and shared in so many Black History Month events. Black History Month is an opportunity to bring all people together, families and friends, Black and white, young and old, to learn more about each other and try our best to keep those relationships growing, developing and working together. Black History Month has given me opportunities to travel all over the country, meeting so many good people trying to make our community a better place. I would like to take this opportunity to express my appreciation to several people who inspired and encouraged me to keep doing my work over the years: the late Len Garrison who was based in Nottingham at that time, an educationalist and historian

100

who gave me much encouragement to continue my work; Don Kinch who is based in Birmingham, and a respected playwright and director, who taught me about theatre workshops; Thomas Baptiste who is an established Black actor in major theatres in the West End and films, who shared with me his early experiences and that of others who came to England looking for work as young Black actors and actresses in the early 50s; the late Wolde Selassie, Leicester's poet and community activist who gave me one of the greatest compliments towards my work by saying that I was one of the most prolific artists of my generation to come out of Leicester; Carol Leeming a dear friend and respected artist, one of Leicester's many great singers and poets who was there from my humble beginnings and always encouraged me; Herdle White, BBC Radio Leicester's longstanding presenter and good friend was instrumental in helping me to establish my play as a radio play in 1998 with BBC Radio Leicester and with other radio networks throughout the country; and the late Biddy Roberts Warwickshire artists team in Leamington Spa who fought long and hard for me to get into schools.

Black History Month, 30 years, is it long or short? In terms of technology, how much of our world has evolved in the last 30 years? When I started to do my theatre business 21 years ago, I didn't have a computer. All correspondence with my clients was by post or phone. I was excited when I got my first fax machine! Technology has changed drastically since then. The way of communication has changed completely. Social media is one of the most important ways to find information

101

Victor Richards. *Streets Paved with Gold.*
Photographer Suleman Garcia.

and connect with other people. Many of the art formats have become digital. YouTube is a huge method to put our creative work out into the world. However, most importantly, learning more about our African and African Caribbean people's achievement and contribution to the rest of the world has had a massive impact in our community in improving better awareness of equality of opportunities and increasing diversity. This is something we should be proud of and worth celebrating. It's my dream to continue my work and continue to inspire new generations for another 30 years.

Leicester is one of the most diverse cities in the UK. Students come to Leicester's universities from all over the world. Leicester City Football Club became Premier League champions in 2016. I am very proud of that, when I travelled to Japan last year, it's one of the first things people mentioned.

Finally, I'd like to thank Pawlet Brookes, Executive Artistic Director of Serendipity for giving me this opportunity to share my view on Black History Month celebrations and for the opportunity she gave me in the past at the Peepul Centre when she was the Artistic Director there.

Krissi Bohn, *The Bogus Woman.* Photographer Mathew Foster, photograph reproduced with permission of Mama Quilla.

JULIE D SMITH

BLACK HISTORY MONTH BELONGS TO EVERYONE

First of all, I would like to express my gratitude for the opportunity to celebrate. I was born and raised in the UK, but where I grew up I don't remember Black history ever being celebrated. At school I was never taught about my heritage, my history, and that is exactly what it is - my history. It was in Leicester I started my journey of learning my own history through going to events and then eventually organising events.

I came to Leicester in 1991 to study for a degree in dance at Leicester Polytechnic, and graduated in 1994. It was at that time it became De Montfort University, and it was great just being involved in the arts within Leicester. After graduating, I became one of the directors for New Works, a festival set up for emerging artists. I also worked for Leicester City Council and East Midlands Arts. At that time, they had a post going for a dance development worker, based at the African Caribbean Centre, and my remit was all about dance and developing African Caribbean dance in Leicester. Earle Robinson was the arts development worker so I worked with Earle and it was also around that time that I became more aware of Black History Month. I would go out and talk to the community, set up workshops and teacher training days.

Before coming to Leicester, I didn't really know much about Black history, apart from my family's background history, which was very personal to me being a Black person and just growing up. I didn't come across it in school or anything. I suppose the only thing that I can really remember is when the series 'Roots' came out, which was kind of revolutionary because it was on TV and it was great. However, looking back on that now,

it instilled the idea that for Black people the only part of their history was slavery, and there were a lot of negative connotations. I was born in the UK, and I'm very western, but you know I am a proud Black British woman and that doesn't mean that I am not interested to know where I have come from, and the people that have allowed me to be who I am. Growing up I had no idea about the history of Black people. I knew the history of slaves, of Black people as slaves, but I didn't know the history of Black people. If there was anything else on the TV it was usually negative, not much positivity.

I can't remember if it was directly with Black History Month but for some of the workshops we organised, we got Jackie Guy to come and do work with the tutors that were already here for continued professional development around dance. We also got a company over that were called Passo O Passo and we worked with a group of people in the community to prepare them as a troupe for the carnival.

I was on the committee for Black History Month with Carol Leeming, Donna Jackman and Earle Robinson, and I listened to Herdle White on the BBC. In the late 90s, early 2000, I worked for Midlands Arts Marketing, who were the marketing and research agency for the East Midlands, and there was a regional Black History Month brochure that I was involved in pulling together. It was quite interesting at that time because there was a lot of stuff happening in Leicester, and a few bits and pieces happening in Nottingham, but there wasn't really anything happening in Derby or Northampton. It was definitely Leicester and Nottingham that were organising the majority of events: food, talks, performances, poetry, etc.

I can remember going to an Achievement Awards at the African Caribbean Centre in Leicester and Elvy Morton getting her award, and she said something that really stuck with me. Elvy said that when she first came to this country there were signs on the doors 'No Blacks, No Irish and No Dogs'. She said that there were a group of people who she wanted to thank as well, and that was the Polish. She said that she had a neighbour or something like that, and they kind of stuck together. That struck me for some reason, and I don't know why, perhaps because of the issues about immigration at the moment, and the negative things being said about Polish people, and it reminded me of what Elvy said about the Polish community.

I also worked alongside Pawlet Brookes, when the Peepul Centre was still being built. We did a lot of off-site arts projects in the lead-up to it opening. I think it was part of Black History Month and we did an event at a restaurant, called 'Rum Punch and Poets' event, which was brilliant. The restaurant did the food, Pawlet made the rum punch, and Jean 'Binta' Breeze performed her poetry, it was a relaxed evening of entertainment, food and drink.

I suppose that in terms of what Serendipity are doing now, it's still pushing to bring Black arts to the forefront of mainstream theatres and festivals, and getting them to include Black arts in their programmes, which has always been a struggle. In terms of history, Black history, I do think that it is important as a Black community that we need to push forward and get our history and our stories told. That's why Black History Month is important. It's important because we can focus on the history around that month and celebrate that history, and use that as a basis for more things happening throughout the year. I think that as a Black community we need to share our knowledge somehow maybe a regular Black history session or discussion session, where you could go away and research and then come back and share what you've learnt. Black History Month belongs to everyone in whatever way we want to celebrate and that we should be allowed to do that. There needs to be a programme of history, a programme on what people are doing within the arts, food, a mash up of everything.

I also think it's important that we record these different histories and memories, if we don't then they will get lost. We are making history, and that should be archived because there are so many things that have been lost throughout the years regarding Black people and our history. We need to start recording them and getting them written down.

So what does Black History Month mean to me? It's about remembrance, celebration and learning. Remembering those that made an important contribution to how we as a human race live, celebrating those past and present, and learning about the past and present, so that we as a community have a shared history for those that follow. Do we still need a Black History Month? If the history of Black people was being integrated into everyday history then no, we don't. But I must say that I am proud to live in a city that does celebrate the achievements that Black people have made and still make to the UK, and if it wasn't for Black History Month, I wouldn't know about my history. So thank you Leicester!

105

THE BIBI CREW IN ASSOCIATION WITH THEATRE ROYAL

ASSOCIATION WITH THEATRE ROYAL STRATFORD EAST PRESENTS

BiBi Crew
in on a level

May 13th-
June 12th
THEATRE ROYAL
STRATFORD EAST

Choice
96.9 FM

JOURNAL

The BiBi Crew on a Level *(1992)*. Theatre royal Stratford East. Courtesy of Theatre Royal Stratford East Archives.

CON-
TEMPO-
RARY
VOICES

a Lopez performing *Silent Aria*, music composed by *Philip Herbert* and choreography by *Henri Oguike*, art of *Black History Month 2013*. Photographer Tom Simpson.

TARA LOPEZ

A TAKE ON BLACK HISTORY MONTH

As I try to think back to the first time I heard the words 'Black History Month' I really struggle – perhaps I would have heard it on the news, or maybe I would have seen signs for Black History Month events in venues; the truth is I have no idea. What is easier to pinpoint, however, is when I first took note of what Black History Month was and when I first became involved; it was when I was studying at De Montfort University and began volunteering for Leicester based arts organisation Serendipity.

It was 2012 and having just begun my second year of university as a Dance student I was keen to get involved in arts events across the city. BHM Live was an event taking place at Curve Theatre to showcase the work of emerging Black artists and as a volunteer I helped out at the event and was also able to watch and view the performances, presentations and exhibitions as an audience member.

Since then I have probably attended a handful of different Black History Month events from concerts to exhibitions and discussions but the question of what I think of Black History Month itself is something very different to what I think of these individual events.

If I take things back a few paces; I grew up in a mixed household – my father was born in Jamaica and moved to London aged 13, my mother is English born and raised in Surrey. I have two older siblings of Black Jamaican heritage, and two other older siblings of dual-heritage. Whilst our family life was always full of colour (in every sense of the word), as I look back I realise that life outside of our home didn't always reflect this. Going to school I was definitely a minority – there were perhaps

a handful of other children who were non-white British. Our school curriculum, particularly history, focused heavily on white British history – in fact I don't ever recall seeing a Black face or character in any history book or English book I ever had to study. I do remember studying the movie version of Shakespeare's *'Much Ado About Nothing'* starring Denzel Washington but that really is about it. I suppose the point I am trying to make here is that school curriculum seemed white-washed, and not that I necessarily felt so at the time (how would I have known the difference?) but certainly from where I stand now I can see where people and places were skipped over or ignored.

So, what does this mean? Well, for me, it meant that any links with my Caribbean cultural heritage had to be sought outside of school and whilst some of this came from my family, my strongest connection to Caribbean culture as a child was definitely our annual trip to Notting Hill Carnival. This held such importance for me as a child and I remember the excitement I would feel as I got out of the tube station with my family and was met with the smells of hot Caribbean food, the beautiful colours of the costumes and the bone shaking vibrations from the sound systems. A chicken *pattie* and chunks of sugar cane were the treat I had dreamed of the whole journey to the event and I was never disappointed. Other memories of Caribbean culture throughout childhood are strongly based around food and music – singing and dancing to reggae in our sitting room on a Sunday when Dad was off work and having the only meal ever cooked by dad... dumplings with bacon (which I'm sure he had us children believing were his own invention).

107

As a young adult at university I began attending different cultural events and venues through university studies and my eyes were opened beyond my own interpretation of Caribbean and British Black culture (dancing to reggae, carnival and Dad's dumplings) to include historical references such as Empire Windrush, and people I had never heard of before but instantly fascinated and inspired me like Josephine Baker, Sarah Baartman or even living legends such as H Patten. As I began to learn more I found myself insanely frustrated that I had spent at least 19 years of my life not knowing these people or understanding the history of both my English and Caribbean heritage. In order to ease this frustration, I began to research, and research, and research some more, and what I find out, to this day, continues to inspire and astonish me.

So, where does this leave Black History Month within my own experience? In all honesty as I sit here typing and contemplating, I'd have to say... nowhere. Black History Month has not been the catalyst for me to learn about my cultural heritage or to understand more about different cultures and communities. This has come from my own curiosity, my love for my own beautifully mixed up heritage and the inspirational individuals who I am lucky enough to have met and learnt about along the way.

This makes me question what the intention of Black History Month is? If it is to educate people about different cultures and forgotten or white washed histories then honestly it's not doing its job and in one month out of 12 it never could, but, if the whole point is to inspire more people to want to find out about their heritage or other cultures and communities, then that is a concept I can wholly support.

There is so much culture and diversity out there and until education in this country becomes truly reflective of our multi-cultural make-up then unfortunately many more people will have to make their own journey to answers, just as I have. This isn't how it should be and it certainly isn't how I'd like to see things when I have my own children someday, so rather than seeing Black History Month as the only time when such cultures are celebrated and given a platform – I wish to see Black History Month used to open up everyone's eyes to the wealth of incredible history, other cultures, forgotten places in history and the wonderful culturally diverse talent that exists today.

If we can use Black History Month to do this on all levels, from the children in school who aren't represented in current curriculum, to the people of influence within education – then I would hope to see a day where a month named 'Black History Month' is unnecessary and obsolete because we are living and breathing all history, all races and ethnicities, and all cultures every day of our lives.

BOSTON 'THE ORATOR' WILLIAMS

EVERY DAY WE REWRITE HISTORY UNTIL IT REFLECTS OURSTORY

Black History Month should be the annual culmination of and expression of Black love, and Black power within the UK. Black History Season, Black History Month, whatever the politics around its duration may be — it should only ever be the culmination of Black history that continues to be written daily. I don't believe Black History Month should be necessary in 2017 but the reality dictates that there may be swathes of people, Black and otherwise, that would be none the wiser to names such as Steve Biko, Fred Hampton, Angela Davis or Edward Juba. The relevance and reach of Black History Month is often brought into contention when spoke upon in barber shops, community centres and the streets. I see it as a topic that provokes, as well as promotes, passionate discussion — has any good ever come out of these discussions? Yes, without an ounce of doubt. The national mood or attitude towards Black History Month may never be commanded by the Black people of the UK, and that's no loss to us insofar we continue to educate and inform our own through education, peer example and barbershop discussion. I couldn't write about Black History Month without perpetuating the cliché — EVERY DAY is Black History Day, EVERY DAY we forge Black history, EVERY DAY we rewrite HIStory until it reflects OURstory. When we realise that our actions today is the history of tomorrow, we'll know that we wield the power of Black history and Black future in this very moment.

I can't not help but believe that Black History Month should be an annual culmination and expression of Black love and Black power in the UK. According to the Institute of Race Relations in 2014 'Black Groups' made up 3.4% of the UK, excluding Asian and other types of Black and Minority Ethnic groups. Some may argue that such small contingent of people should not have such a large voice in the cultural and social shaping of an 87.2% 'White British' country. My experiences show that on a social level and arts and cultural level we do have great say in determining what is 'cool' or 'in'. We don't have this same clout in the political and economic sectors. Now until we as a people have equal and fair opportunity to increase our economic and political clout then we must continue to shout about our rich history, which continues to be written up until this present moment. We must show and shout about our greatness from the rooftops... just to be heard. Such is the tale of being a Black person in the UK, work twice as hard for half the reward. Black History Month should be our collective howl, a blistering racket about how awesome and great we are — without this collective howl we risk being forgotten by the country we call home during the one month the country is open to hearing our history as described by our narrative.

Above all we must celebrate Black History Month for ourselves. More important than being heard by the nation is the preservation of our cultures. Second and third generation Caribbean young people are two to three steps removed from the lands, languages and nuances that define our cultures. Celebration of these things even just once a year is an opportunity to ensure the next generation does not forget the roots of the cultures they continue to define today.

"When I was in school, being African was a diss" – Skepta (as featured alongside Drake in Wizkid's 'Ojuelegba', 2015). This rang true during my time at school also. From year 10 onwards I had a bit more sense and would shut down anybody perpetuating ignorance around me. Isn't that crazy though? I was 15 before I stopped seeing being African as an acceptable disrespect. I don't think I'm alone in that, I hope that kind of thinking dies out soon.

One of my most cherished experiences regarding Black History Month has to be the FeVsMale event held in Birmingham. The event was full to the rafters, the essence of the event was male artists vs female artists with the crowd deciding which team won. I went back to back with a female poet called Najite Phoenix - her work is powerful, describing stories of Black female triumph, her cadence is smooth and gentle, she had been around for years and knew how to work a crowd. Each poem she delivered received a rapturous applause. I held my own and matched her reception each round. It was the first time I had a wheel up on a poem, 'I Know What Women Want' had the mandem/gentlemen going crazy. It was so beautiful to see people on their feet screaming out 'brap! brap! brap!' pointing gun fingers in the air in response to streams of words about Black love and cultural taboos. That night was life. Good people, good vibes and it felt nice to be in a 95% black environment.

We're 30 years gone, the next 30 years are ours to define. I feel like the collective voice of the Black British people is swelling up to what may become a bellowing roar. We're more connected than ever, we've got access to information at the click of a button, we can disseminate that information with just another click. Black History Month can reach more people than ever, we can have more people contributing to the dialogue than ever - keeping alive the cultures of the diaspora.

Black History Month for all its criticisms is important. It's an opportunity to rave and shout about our awesomeness, it's an opportunity to keep the third generation Black British young people clued up on the depth of the diaspora they belong to. Keep shouting – keep being great – keep being defiantly Black.

Power to my people.

Boston *'The Orator'* **Williams.** Photographer Aglana.

MILESTONES

1765 TO 2017 A LOCAL AND NATIONAL PICTURE OF BLACK HISTORY

The contents of this timeline aim to highlight some of the key events in Black history over the last 250 years, and also reflect upon how national and international events have shaped local Black history, and how local events have contributed to the national and international picture. The facts documented here do not seek to be a complete history, but a point of reference for reflection and further research. Acknowledging the often under told, or untold contributions of the African and African Caribbean community.

112

Mary Seacole *(circa 1873).*
Photographer Maull and Company, London.

DATE	NATIONAL AND INTERNATIONAL EVENTS	LEICESTER EVENTS
1765	The start of the campaign for emancipation of slaves in Britain.	
1783	British withdrawal from America, following the War of Independence, brings loyalists to Britain, including a small number of Black slaves who had been promised freedom if they fought for Britain.	
1787	Population of 20,000 Black people in London.	
1789	Publication of the memoirs of Olaudah Equiano – 'The Interesting Narratives of the life of Olaudah Equiano' – the main spokesman for Britain's Black community.	
1750 – 1807	William Wilberforce (1759 – 1833) an abolitionist who came from a prosperous merchant family of Kingston-Upon-Hull. In 1787 he became the leader of the abolition movement.	Thomas Babington (1758 – 1837) the eighth and last Babington to hold the family manor of Rothley with its centre at Rothley Temple in Leicestershire. He spent two of his years at Cambridge with William Wilberforce, forging a lifelong friendship, blossoming into a very productive team in the Abolitionist cause. Babington hosted Wilberforce at Rothley with others where they would plan their various campaigns to make Britain a more moral society. In 1800 Babington became one of Leicester's two MPs, enabling him to support Wilberforce in the successful passing of the Bill to Abolish the Slave Trade in 1807.
1791 – 1804	A slave uprising in St Domingue in 1791 sets off the Haitian Revolution, led by Toussaint L'Ouverture with an army of ex-slaves. The revolution eventually leads to St Domingue becoming independent Haiti in 1804. On January 1, St Domingue is declared the republic of Haiti, the first independent Black state outside Africa.	
1807	The Act to Abolish the Slave Trade was passed by British Parliament.	
1824 – 1825	Actor Ira Aldridge (1807 - 1867), the only Black actor to be awarded with a bronze plaque at the Shakespeare Memorial Theatre, makes his UK debut at London's Royal Coburg Theatre.	Leicester abolitionist Elizabeth Heyrick (1769 - 1831) a strong supporter for complete emancipation, publishes the influential pamphlet *Immediate, not Gradual Abolition*.
1831	Mary Prince becomes the first published Black female author in the UK with her autobiography, *The History of Mary Prince*.	

DATE	NATIONAL AND INTERNATIONAL EVENTS	LEICESTER EVENTS
1833	The Slavery Abolition Act was passed by British Parliament.	
1855	Mary Seacole opens her British Hotel near the British camp, nursing soldiers fighting in the Crimean war.	
1909	*Lily of Bermuda*, Britain's first African Caribbean theatrical production is staged in Manchester by playwright and actor Ernest Trimingham.	
1913	John Richard Archer (1863-1932), Britain's first Black councillor also becomes Britain's first Black mayor of Battersea. Born in Liverpool in 1863, he was a photographer by profession, and was elected first president of the African Progress Union.	
1914 – 1918	British West Indies Regiment decorated after World War One with some of the highest awards. Sixteen servicemen from the West African Frontier Force and the King's African Rifles were awarded Distinguished Conduct Medals. The role of Africans as Carrier Corps was vital in the East Africa campaign against the Germans. Walter Daniel Tull, a Black professional footballer with Tottenham Hotspur, joined up before conscription in 1915. He gained his commission in May 1917 and became the first Black commissioned officer in the British army. He died in 1918, aged 30, on a battlefield near Favreuil in France. Caribbean men conscripted to serve in World War One • 10280 Jamaica • 1478 Trinidad and Tobago • 831 Barbados • 700 British Guyana • 445 Grenada • 229 Leeward Islands • 2137 from other islands.	 **West Indian Regiment** reproduced with permission of Leicester Museums and Galleries.
1918	Birth of Nelson Mandela.	
1926	Negro History Week founded by Carter G. Woodson	
1930		Canadian boxer Larry Gains known as the 'The Toronto Terror' moves to Leicester From 1930-1937 he wins 17 out of 18 fights including one against heavyweight champion of the British Empire, Phil Scott, at the Tigers ground on Welford Road in front of a crowd of around 34,000.

DATE	NATIONAL AND INTERNATIONAL EVENTS	LEICESTER EVENTS

1939 – 1945

More than 200,000 Africans and 6,000 Caribbeans fought in World War Two. Around 300 men from the Caribbean enlisted in the RAF for aircrew duties, and some 5,500 volunteered for ground duties. More than 600 Caribbean women volunteered to join the Auxiliary Territorial Service (ATS) - 300 of those volunteers spent the war years in the Caribbean, 200 were posted to the United States, and 100 were stationed in Britain. The crews of the merchant ships which kept Britain supplied during both World Wars included many African, Caribbean, Indian and Chinese seamen. Many went down in ships torpedoed by U-boats.

Una Marson (1905-1965) becomes the first Black female broadcaster at the BBC from 1939 to 1946. Establishing *Calling the West Indies* (later *Caribbean Voices*).

Larry Gains judges a Fancy dress carnival St Chad Shrove Tuesday *(1932)*. Photograph reproduced with permission of Elaine Smith, Churchwarden at St Chads Church.

1944

Race riots between Black and White American service men on the streets of Leicester.

1948

British Nationality Act gives all Commonwealth people right to British Citizenship.

MV (Monte Rosa – passenger liner and cruise ship launched in Germany in 1930) Empire Windrush brings the first wave of Caribbean migrants to Britain.

West Indian Sports and Cultural Club established in Leicester.

1950

Immigration from Commonwealth to Britain from Ireland, Caribbean, South Asia, Italy and Cyprus.

Cy Grant sings the news in Calypso on British TV on the Tonight Programme.

1951

Earl Cameron stars in *Pool of London*, becoming one of the first Black actors to appear in a starring role in British film. *Pool of London* also portrayed the first interracial relationship in a British film.

1952

Trinidadian sprinter Emmanuel MacDonald Bailey is first Black athlete to win an Olympic medal competing for Great Britain (he won a bronze medal in the 100 metres at the Helsinki Olympic Games).

DATE	NATIONAL AND INTERNATIONAL EVENTS	LEICESTER EVENTS
1955		Billy Eckstine performs at De Montfort Hall in April.
1956		Lionel Hampton Orchestra performs at De Montfort Hall.
1957		Leicester Caribbean Cricket Club established.
		Sister Rosetta Tharpe Performs at De Montfort Hall
1958	West Indies Federation formed.	
	Trinidadian Edric Connor becomes first Black actor to perform with the Royal Shakespeare Company.	
	Moon on a Rainbow Shawl by actor and playwright Errol John premieres at the Royal Court.	
1959		George Lewis New Orleans Jazz Band and Louis Armstrong perform at De Montfort Hall (January and March respectively)
		Singer Sarah Vaughan and Dizzy Gillespie perform at De Montfort Hall (January and November respectively).
1960	A TV drama called The Dark Man stars Earl Cameron as a West Indian cab driver. It tries to honestly examine the reactions and prejudices he faces at work.	
1961	Derby West Indian Association formed.	Jazz legends Art Blakely, John Coltrane and Miles Davis perform at De Montfort Hall (in April and November.)
1962	Commonwealth Immigrants Act passed, introducing an employment voucher system restricting entry to skilled and professional people.	Ella Fitzgerald and Count Basie perform at De Montfort Hall (February and April, respectively)
	Jamaica becomes the first Caribbean island to gain independence from Britain.	
	Nelson Mandela arrested and sentenced to five years in prison for leaving the country without a passport and incitement.	
1963	The UK TV show, Tonight has an episode narrated by George Lamming. It's a poetic and impressionistic view of Black working class life in Britain.	
	USA invades Grenada and assassinates Prime Minister, Maurice Bishop.	

116

DATE	NATIONAL AND INTERNATIONAL EVENTS	LEICESTER EVENTS
1964	First Notting Hill Carnival Nelson Mandela was sentenced to life imprisonment as he was convicted of sabotage. BBC One documentary, *The Colony*, filmed in Birmingham, gives a voice to working class Caribbean settlers.	Elaine Hinds becomes Leicester first Black telephonist for the Leicester General Post Office.
1965	The Race Relations Act passed was the first legislation in the United Kingdom to address racial discrimination. The Act outlawed discrimination on the "grounds of colour, race, or ethnic or national origins" in public places. BBC One airs *Fable*, a drama by John Hopkins in which apartheid is reversed. With a cast including Thomas Baptiste, Rudolph Walker and Carmen Munroe.	Cy Grant (who sang a calypso version of the news on the BBC) plays Othello at Phoenix Theatre in Leicester.
1966	Malcolm X assassinated. Local Government Act provides funding for local authorities to help ethnic minority groups. First Black Officer, Norwell Roberts, joins London's Metropolitan Police Force. The Caribbean Artists Movement is founded in London. It oversees and protects the literary, academic and performance skills of Caribbean writers and artists. Andrew Salkey, Edward Kamau Brathwaite and John La Rose were the catalysts. *Jemima + Johnny* directed by South African Lionel Ngakane premieres. The first world Black and African Festival of Arts and Culture takes place in Dakar.	Jamaica Community Service Group established in Leicester.

DATE	NATIONAL AND INTERNATIONAL EVENTS	LEICESTER EVENTS
1967	*Rainbow City* airs on BBC One, starring Errol John as a Jamaican lawyer living in Birmingham. E.R. Braithwaite's novel *To Sir, With Love* about his experiences as a teacher in the East End of London gets made into a film with Sidney Poitier. A renowned writer, lecturer and a representative for the UN, Braithwaite was born in Guyana. It was his London teaching and social work (finding foster homes for non-white kids) that provided him with the material for his eloquent and moving stories about race and class in Britain. Robert Lawrence was selected by the USAF for the Air Force's Manned Orbital Laboratory (MOL) program, becoming the first Black astronaut.	
1968	Basil D'Oliviera not selected for cricket tour by England to apartheid South Africa. Martin Luther King assassinated. Barbara Blake Hannah is the first Black on camera reporter on *Today wth Eamonn Andrews*.	
1969	Sir Learie Constantine becomes the first Black peer in the House of Lords. *The Roar of the Crowd* on BBC Two - a series in which sports stars talk about themselves features cricketer 'Six sixes in one over-Gary Sobers'. The Jamaican, Frank Cousins creates the Dark and Light Theatre - the first Black theatre in Britain to receive government funding and have its own building. They create their own touring circuit and stage plays from America, Africa, the Caribbean and Britain including Blood Knot, The Trials of Brother Jero and The Slave. Desmond Dekker is the first Jamaican to have a no.1 single in Britain with 'Israelites'.	The Herdle White Show on BBC Radio Leicester commenced.
1970		Highfields Rangers were formed in 1970.
1971	MGM Studios releases *Shaft*	Leicester Afro-Caribbean Business Association was formed in 1971.

DATE	NATIONAL AND INTERNATIONAL EVENTS	LEICESTER EVENTS
1972	*Love Thy Neighbour* begins broadcasting on ITV. Focusing on the relationship between white and Black neighbours. Temba Theatre Company, the first Black British Theatre Company, is founded by Alton Kumalo and Oscar James.	
1973	Trevor McDonald joins ITN as a reporter from the BBC World Service and becomes Britain's first Black TV news reporter.	Leicester Caribbean Credit Union Ltd and Leicester Afro-Caribbean Cultural Arts were formed. Grass Roots Dance Company formed.
1974		Contrast Steel Band and Leicester United Caribbean Association formed.
1975	Lenny Henry makes his television debut winning the New Faces talent competition by doing stand-up comedy impersonations. *Pressure* directed by Horace Ové is released, widely regarded as the first Black British feature film, focusing on issues faced by British-born Caribbean young people.	
1976	Race Relations Act extends the scope of earlier legislation to cover indirect racism. Commission for Racial Equality established, following the foundations laid by the Community Relations Council. CRE was a non-departmental public body in the United Kingdom, which aimed to address racial discrimination and promote racial equality. Its work has been merged into the new Equality and Human Rights Commission. *The Fosters*, the first British sitcom to have an all Black cast airs on ITV. *The Arts Britain Ignores* was a ground-breaking report written by Naseem Khan. This was the first report to highlight the cultural work of ethnic minority communities in Britain.	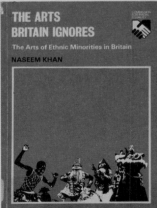 **The Arts Britain Ignores** by Naseem Kahn.

DATE	NATIONAL AND INTERNATIONAL EVENTS	LEICESTER EVENTS
1976	Minority Arts Advisory Service established. Singer, actor, Black activist Paul Robeson dies at the age of 78. His 11 films included Body And Soul, Jericho and Proud Valley. Black History Month begins in February in the USA.	
1977	*Roots* hits television screens, based on Alrx Haley's 1976 novel. Roots: The Saga of an American Family. This series focused on slavery, the abolition of slavery in America and affected the Black community in the UK as it showed negative stories and ancestral connections relating to Black history. The Second World Black African Festival of Arts and Culture takes place in Nigeria, the largest pan-African gathering of its time to take place.	Clifton Robinson appointed as deputy chairman of the Commission for Racial Equality. After serving in the Royal Air Force from 1944, then teaching in Kingston, Jamaica, he came back to Britain in 1951 and taught at Mellor Primary School in Leicester. He later became the first Black head teacher in Britain, and Leicester's first Black JP. He was awarded the OBE and the CBE for his work in education and the community.
1978	First Black soap opera, *Empire Road*, on British TV, addressing Britain's growing multi-cultural society. *Mixed Blessings* airs on ITV, centres on the life of a newlywed couple, Thomas Simpson, who is white, and Susan Lambert, who is Black. Lambeth Council establishes Britain's first race relations unit. Viv Anderson becomes the first Black footballer to be picked for the England squad.	Carved ivory mask, Benin, Nigeria used as the symbol of FESTAC '77 Copyright © The Trustees of the British Museum
1979	Arthur Lewis become the first Black economics professor in Britain.	Raddle Books was founded on Melbourne Road, Highfields.
1980	Ronald Hope becomes the first Black police inspector in Britain. Seminal film, *Babylon* by Franco Rosso is released. Roland Butcher becomes the first Black cricketer to play for England .	Laurel Aitken popularised Ska music in 1950s and he enjoyed the resurgence of Ska music in the wake of the 2 Tone movement (Ska revival music genre led by Jerry Dammers and The Specials). He had success with the UK Singles Chart with "Rudi Got Married". Aitken's career also focused on mento/calypso, R&B, Ska, rock steady, and reggae, and in the 1990s he even turned his talents to dancehall.

DATE	NATIONAL AND INTERNATIONAL EVENTS	LEICESTER EVENTS
1981	'Sus Law' was originally created and brought into force in 1824 as the Vagrancy Act. However, in the 1970s it was widely used primarily as a means of policing Black youth by the UK police force. Under the 'Sus Law', or 'stop and search', 'every person or reputed thief, frequenting or loitering about in a street highway or avenue leading thereto or any place of public resort with intent to commit and arrestable offence is guilty of that offence.' Police were empowered to stop and search citizens without burden of proof merely on the basis of suspicion ('sus') that they intended to commit a crime. The 'Sus Law' was widely regarded among the Black communities to be a form of legalised victimisation: not only did it license policemen to persecute Black communities with little or no evidential justification, but it created an atmosphere of alienation among young Blacks, who were made to feel like perpetual suspects in their own neighbourhoods. British Nationality Act passed "to reduce future sources of primary immigration." Black Cultural Archives was founded in 1981, and its mission to collect, preserve and celebrate the heritage and history of Black people in Britain. Moira Stuart becomes the BBC's first Black female newsreader.	Riots in Leicester started in July in the City Centre and Highfields areas. The UK Government following the 1981 Brixton riots commissioned the Scarman report. Lord Scarman was appointed by Home Secretary William Whitelaw on 14 April 1981 (two days after the rioting ended) to hold the enquiry into the riots. The Scarman report was published on 25 November 1981. The Scarman Report found that the disorders were not premeditated, but originated spontaneously as a reaction to what was seen as police harassment. Despite the strong racial element in the disorders, the Report discarded the argument that they were racial riots and concluded that they were essentially an outburst of anger and resentment by Black youths against the police. Highfields Workshop Centre was formed. The Ajani Centre and Afro-Caribbean Education Working Group (ACE) were formed.
1982	Channel 4 aired for the first time with a radically different structure from the three existing channels. It had a remit to cater for youth and minority groups. The government also gave the go-ahead for satellite television.	Caribbean Community Enterprise and The Spectrum Organisation were formed. *Talking Blues*, BBC Radio Leicester's first dedicated programme for the African Caribbean community, begins airing.
1983	*No Problem!* Channel 4's first comedy series begins airing, specifically to address the lifestyle of the British Black community. Its cast were members of the Black Theatre Co-operative which staged plays and included Judith Jacob and Victor Romero Evans. Set in Willesden Green, it was about the grown up Powell children after their parents had returned to Jamaica. The comedy dealt with their lives and ambitions from modelling to running a pirate radio station.	The Caribbean population of Spinney Hill in 1983 was 293 and total population of Caribbean population across all Leicester's wards was at 2,510. Leicester Expressive Arts founded to support arts and culture.

DATE	NATIONAL AND INTERNATIONAL EVENTS	LEICESTER EVENTS
1984	The 1984 Police and Criminal Evidence Act included a clause that instructed the police that they now had to give a reason why they had stopped someone.	Leicester Caribbean Carnival Committee was formed, founders included Elvy Morton.
1985	November 2, 1985, Reverend Jesse Jackson joined with Oliver Tambo, Bishop Trevor Huddleston, Ken Livingstone, Bernie Grant, Keith Vaz, Paul Boateng, Diane Abbot and others at the 120,000 strong demonstration in London's Trafalgar Square to protest against apartheid in South Africa and call on the South African government to free Nelson Mandela. He later met with Prime Minister Margaret Thatcher, appealing to her to drop Britain's support for apartheid. Wilfred Wood becomes the first Black bishop in the Church of England, overseeing the Diocese of Southwark.	Afro Caribbean and Asian Forum were formed. Leicester's first Caribbean Carnival took place.
1986	Between 1983 and 1986 British imports of South African textiles and clothing fell by 35%. In June 1986 an opinion poll found that 27% of people in Britain boycotted South African products.	Nelson Mandela Park was formerly known as Welford Road Recreation Ground but was renamed Nelson Mandela Park on 6 August 1986. Caribbean Focus Year – Leicester had the biggest range of activities in the country. Earle Robinson awarded the MBE for services to community education.
1987	A turning point in Black British politics occurred with the first three Black MPs elected to Parliament in 1987, Bernie Grant, Labour MP for Tottenham, 1987-2000, Paul Boateng, Labour MP for Brent South, 1987-2005 and Diane Abbott, Labour MP for Hackney North and Stoke Newington, 1987- Present. Britain in the 1980s was in turmoil in the Thatcher era with the after-effects of the riots in Brixton, Tottenham and Toxteth. Black Britons were fighting for tolerance and acceptance, and against marginalisation, racism and also trying to define a sense of identity and purpose. This was the context behind the development of Black History Month in the UK and Leicester.	 **Sisters of the Long March (1988)** Image reproduced with permission of Ross Galbraith

122

DATE	NATIONAL AND INTERNATIONAL EVENTS	LEICESTER EVENTS
1987	Richard Stokes becomes first Black man to join Royal Guards. Diane Abbott becomes the first Black woman elected to the British Parliament. Black History Month was formally first celebrated in the UK, in London through the leadership of Ghanaian analyst Akyaaba Addai-Sebo and Greater London Council (GLC). On the first official Black History Month event on the 1 October 1987, Dr. Maulana Karenga was invited as the first speaker as a result of being the originator of Kwanzaa, which was a successful part of the cultural calendar both in the USA and the UK. The event held every October celebrates traditional values and African history as part of its cultural and religious programme. The African Jubilee Year Declaration was launched in 1987, which called on local and national government to recognise the contributions of Africans to the cultural, economic and political life of London and the UK.	Joseph Allen becomes first African Caribbean elected member of Leicester City Council. In Highfield's area of Leicester, there was a campaign to boycott all South African goods. Talking Blues Support Group and Provision for Afro-Caribbean Elderly (PACE) were formed. Donald Eugene Cherry was an American jazz trumpeter and performed at Haymarket Theatre in Leicester in 1987. Linda Herbert is recognised by Leicester Society of Jamaicans. Highfields Rangers become the first non-London side to win a competition sponsored by the Caribbean Times Newspaper.
1988	The AAM (Anti-Apartheid Movement) launched the 'Nelson Mandela: Freedom at 70' campaign at a concert in Wembley Stadium in 1988. Rock Stars played to a capacity audience and the BBC broadcasted the concert to over 60 countries. Next day 25 freedom marchers set off from Glasgow for London, where they arrived on the eve of Mandela's birthday. A quarter of a million people gathered in Hyde Park to hear Bishop Desmond Tutu call for Mandela's release. On 18 July a special service was held in St James's Piccadilly and thousands of cards were delivered to South Africa House. Barbados born Jim Braithwaite sets up multi-million pound computer firm, the first Black company to be listed on the Stock Exchange. Leonard Woodley and John Roberts are first Black QCs to take silk.	'Sisters of the Long March' toured Britain, September – December 1988, to win support for South African workers in their long-running dispute with the British-owned company BTR Sarmcol. The Sisters were a seven-woman song and dance group from Natal. They took their show to over 20 venues all over the country. The year before, a theatre group set up by the BTR workers brought their play about the strike 'The Long March' to Britain. Both tours were sponsored by the British TUC and supported by the AAM. Foundation Housing Association established in Leicester.

DATE	NATIONAL AND INTERNATIONAL EVENTS	LEICESTER EVENTS
1989	When Prime Minister Margaret Thatcher undermined international sanctions in the mid - 1980s, the Anti-Apartheid Movement recast the boycott campaign as a call for 'people's sanctions'. In 1989 its Boycott Bandwagon, a converted double-decker bus, took the message to cities and towns all over Britain. *Desmond's* begins airing on Channel 4, set in Peckham, London, it featured a predominantly Black British Guyanese cast. *Ragamuffin* by Amani Napthali premieres at the Oval House.	Two Leicester workers and trade union militants, Ross Galbraith and Gary Sherriff were sacked from Granby Plastics due to their action and demonstrations against a contract to supply goods to South Africa. The order for Nyloil (a plastic substitute for metal) was destined for South Africa. Their sacking initiated a yearlong campaign raising the case for workers' sanctions against apartheid South Africa. Adelaide Hall was an American born UK based Jazz singer and entertainer and she appeared in concert at the Studio Theatre, Haymarket in Leicester. The concert was organised by composer/musician Gavin Bryars and sold out almost as soon as it was announced. *Prime Time* by Nigel Moffet premieres at Haymarket Theatre Leicester.
1990	Sunday 11 February 1990 Nelson Mandela was released from prison. In April 1990 Mandela arrived in London, where he was welcomed at a Wembley concert.	In the early 1990s the Centre for the Study of Public Order was renamed the Scarman Centre for the Study of Public Order in honour of Lord Scarman and his influential observations about public order, policing, civil liberties and social justice in contemporary societies. The Centre carried out a wide range of research projects, including a socio-economic profile and analysis of African Caribbean people in Leicestershire, the policing of football hooliganism, violence against retail staff and policing in central Europe. Striking South African workers from SARMCOL on a tour of the UK participated in an Anti-Poll Tax demonstration in Town Hall Square, Leicester. Leicester Community Radio was formed.
1991	Nelson Mandela was elected ANC (African National Congress) President. The cult youth music programme Dance Energy presented by Normski launches on BBC2 as part of the Def II strand.	African Caribbean Elders Day Centre established in Leicester. The Race Equality Centre in Leicester and Leicestershire (TREC) is founded.

124

DATE	NATIONAL AND INTERNATIONAL EVENTS	LEICESTER EVENTS
1992	Bill Morris becomes the first Black leader of the Transport and General Workers Union, the largest trade union in Britain.	Leicester African Caribbean Business Association formed.
1993	On 22 April 1993, 18-year-old Stephen Lawrence was murdered at a bus stop in Eltham, southeast London. A group of white youths attacked Stephen and he received fatal stab wounds that led to his death. Britain's first Black cable channel, Identity Television launched. Paul Ince becomes first Black player to captain England team.	
1994	On 10 May 1994 Nelson Mandela was inaugurated as South Africa's first democratically elected President.	National Conference of the Association for the Study of African Caribbean and Asian Culture and History in Britain held in Leicester. Highfields Workshop renamed as Imani Ujima Centre.
1995		African Caribbean Citizens Forum established in Leicester. Volcano erupts on Montserrat and a large population was evacuated to the UK and to Leicester.
1996	TV programme *Black Britain* was screened on the BBC. It reflected the lives and experiences of the UK's Black population and was billed as the BBC's first programme specifically for Black viewers. The MOBOs launch and are shown on Channel 4. The awards (for Music of Black Origin) brought a much-needed emphasis to the achievements of Black music and artists.	In 1996 the Scarman Centre for the Study of Public Order was given a new name – the Scarman Centre – and continued to expand its areas of interest and activity. It established new courses in Risk, Crisis and Disaster Management, Emergency Planning and postgraduate studies in Health and Safety. Imani Ujima Centre transferred to the City Council and renamed the African Caribbean Centre in June 1996.
1997	Terry Harrison is awarded an MBE for services to Sport for People with Disabilities in the East Midlands.	Funding ceased in 1997 for the Afro-Caribbean Education Work Group (now known as the Afrikan Caribbean Education Project ACE) Ajani Centre and Raddle books.

DATE	NATIONAL AND INTERNATIONAL EVENTS	LEICESTER EVENTS
1998	The Human Rights Act is a UK law passed in 1998. It lets you defend your rights in UK courts and compels public organisations (including the Government, police and local councils) to treat everyone equally, with fairness, dignity and respect. Julian Henriques film *Babymother* shines a spotlight on Dancehall in the UK.	Black History Month events focus on Windrush story. *Streets Paved with Gold* by Victor Richards performed at The Haymarket, Leicester.
1999		Mainstream Partnership is founded to assist artists from Black and Minority Ethnic communities in the East Midlands to increase their income and employment opportunities as professionals in the mainstream arts sector. October 1999, Black History Month events commemorated African Caribbean achievements and contributions locally, nationally and internationally. Choreographer Sheron Wray choreographed a performance called DNA: Destiny's Natural Ally for Black History Month 1999; performed by dancer Louise Katerega at New Walk Museum in Leicester as part of Vision Re Afrika exhibition.
2000	The Race Relations (Amendment) Act 2000 places a duty on public authorities such as universities and colleges when carrying out their functions to have "due regard" to the need to (a) eliminate unlawful racial discrimination, (b) promote equality of opportunity, and, (c) promote good relations between people of different racial groups.	In October 2000, Black History Month focused on the theme of celebration. Aswad one of Britain's best-loved reggae bands performs at De Montfort Hall in 2000. They have performed in Leicester several times, including 2006, 2017.
2001		Black History Month celebrates the contributions made by Black people in the areas of science, medicine, the arts, the economy and agriculture. In 2001, in Leicester there was a population of 4,610 Black British Caribbean people and 3,432 Black British Africans.
2002		Black History Month events focus on the last five hundred years dominated by slavery, colonialism and the experience of Apartheid in South Africa.

126

DATE	NATIONAL AND INTERNATIONAL EVENTS	LEICESTER EVENTS
2003		Black History Month's theme is "Are We Warriors?" is a fitting tribute to those in the last century who publicised and proclaimed the greatness of the Afrikan world civilisation, and to those before that time whose foresight and ingenuity allowed us to realise our worth in this millennium.
2004	Michael Fuller becomes Britain's first Black Chief Constable in Kent. *Bullet Boy* (2004) directed by Saul Dibb is released.	In 2004, the Scarman Centre was renamed the Department of Criminology and created a BA in Criminology. Black History Month events focused on the theme, 'Liberation' suggesting an escape from confinement. Liberation means in some part to be free from poverty, ignorance, social injustice, alienation and feelings of inferiority. Quest for Liberation has been typified by the work of Marcus Garvey, Kwame Nkrumah, Claudia Jones and a host of other activists.
2005	**Laurel Aitken.** Reproduced with permission of Sandra Aitken and Leicester Mercury	Black History Month explored 'New Beginnings' and along with the traditional programme of Afrocentric experiences, other events have been inspired by the notation of a dawning of a new era, rejuvenation and enrichment. In July, the new Black History Consortium was launched as an independent body in the organisation and development of Black History in the city. The intention was to extend the programme to include Black History experiences, events and activities all year round. Zindzi Mandela opens Peepul Centre in Leicester. Black Future Group founded by Freedom Tariq Zampaladus and Chris Isa. Laurel Aitken died of a heart attack.
2006		The Black History Month theme was the celebration of Black women who have made significant contributions to the social, political, economic and cultural achievements of the city. Women such as Iris Lightfoote who took over as head of the Leicester Racial Equality Council and Jawaahir Daahir who worked hard to build relationships between the Somalian community.

127

DATE	NATIONAL AND INTERNATIONAL EVENTS	LEICESTER EVENTS
2006		Style Up exhibition, a new and innovative exploration of fashion from Leicester's African and African Caribbean Community from 1950s to the present day.
		Rev. Jesse Jackson visits the Peepul Centre, Leicester.
2007		Friday 1 August, the local council held "Nelson Mandela Sports Festival", as a celebration of 21 years of the park having held the name. Important people of the community were present including Councillor Gary Hunt, the Mayor of Leicester. At the event, 21 trees were planted to mark the 21 years of the park and 21 wards of Leicester.
		Mainstream Partnership became a Regularly Funded Organisation (RFO) of Arts Council England in April.
		Historical visits were organised by LACAF June 25 – July 4 2007 as part of Heritage Lottery Leicester Partnership for the commemoration and celebration of the Bicentenary of the Abolition of the African Transatlantic Slave Trade. Visitors included Leicester City Council Chief Executives Office, Princes Trust, SANKOFA Walk, LACBA.
		Black History Month marked the bicentenary of the abolition of the slave trade throughout the British Empire.
		Lorenzo 'Laurel' Aitken known as "Godfather of Ska" an influential Caribbean singer and one of the pioneers of Jamaican Ska music. After a long campaign, a blue plaque, one of 100 blue plaques across Leicestershire commemorating special people, places and events was placed in his honour at his former Leicester home (Munnings Close) in 2007.
2008	On November 4 2008, Barack Obama was elected the first African-American President.	Black History Month celebrated African Renaissance this year. African Renaissance identified African and African Caribbean history and prompted the discovery of past and progressive achievements across the diaspora.
	The slave trade is introduced as part of the history syllabus in the British curriculum.	
2009		Black History Month celebrates 'My History, Our History is Black History' and the discovery of Afrikan written text at Timbuktu Mali.

DATE	NATIONAL AND INTERNATIONAL EVENTS	LEICESTER EVENTS
2010	The Equality Act 2010 replaced anti-discrimination laws with a single Act, making the law easier to understand and strengthening protection in some situations. The Act's provisions are the basic framework of protection against direct and indirect discrimination, harassment and victimisation in services and public functions, work, education, associations and transport.	Serendipity was founded and is a diversity-led organisation with the specific aim of working in partnership with mainstream organisations to put on quality culturally diverse international and national works to audiences across the region as well as nationally. Serendipity's strength lies in its track record of working in the performing arts with venues, producers, promoters, performing arts and media companies and directors who reflect the demographic profile of the UK. Using local, national, international practitioners and artists, Serendipity offers excellence in the arts, ensuring that it not only nurtures new and emerging talent but also showcases the best new work being produced in the sector. Serendipity holds a festival called Lets Dance International Frontiers that supports emerging and international artists.

The Emancipation Project 2010 included a 7 mile Emancipation Walk from Rothley Court to Nelson Mandela Park. This celebrated the freedom of slaves, abolition movement and Nelson Mandela's freedom in South Africa.

Black History Month celebrates the remarkable achievements of Mary Seacole, in the field of nursing, and the local and international Ska music legend, Laurel Aitken. |
| 2011 |

Black History Month Brochure *(2011)* | Black History Month was a tribute to Gil Scott Heron (1 April 1949 - 27 May 2011).

Reverend Jesse Jackson received an honorary degree award from De Montfort University. He also set up a fund called the Rev Jesse Jackson fund of £1,000 that has been introduced to encourage further social cohesion between students and the community. The prize was established to support students or DMU societies to set up projects that will increase cultural integration with the local community or on campus.

Serendipity is awarded the Black History Month tender from Leicester City Council to produce the Black History Month programme for 2012. |

129

DATE	NATIONAL AND INTERNATIONAL EVENTS	LEICESTER EVENTS
2012	The London 2012 Games , its Opening Ceremony and the associated Cultural Olympiad bring worldwide attention to the cultural diversity of the UK.	Ballet Black perform at Curve Theatre, invited by Serendipity, as part of LDIF2012's Cultural Olympiad programme.
		L'Acadco Dance Company from Jamaica perform at Curve as part of Serendipity's Cultural Olympiad programme.
		Black History Month paid tribute to the 50 years of independence for Jamaica, Trinidad and Tobago with Linton Kwesi Johnson, whose words have become part of British history, carving out the relationship between the Caribbean and the reality of the UK.
2013	Nelson Mandela died on December 5, 2013 at the age of 95. The Stuart Hall Project, directed by John Akomfrah, documents the life of cultural activist Stuart Hall and his relationship with Britain.	Temple Education was founded in 2013 by Lois McNab, Joycelyn Harris, and Carmen Gilfillian who introduced Afrikan and Black Studies.
		Black History Month 2013 celebrated the fiftieth anniversary of Martin Luther King's 'I have a dream' speech.
		2013 saw the start of the 'Save Our Season' campaign by Leicester Black History Consortium when the Season was changed back to the Month of celebrations (October) in line with the national picture.
		Jesse Jackson Park off Troon Way, in Rushey Mead was named after the American Civil Rights leader Rev Jesse Jackson who described Leicester as "a beacon for the rest of the world" during his visit to the City on 5 December 2013. His visit marked 50 years since Dr Martin Luther King's march on Washington and famous I have a *Dream* speech. The park was named after the 72-year-old Baptist minister to thank him for his tireless campaigning for race equality and civil rights.
2014		Black History Month 2014 celebrated the accomplishments of Nobel Laureates; Toni Morrison, the first Black woman to receive the Nobel Peace Prize for Literature and Derek Walcott, the first Caribbean writer to receive the honour.
		In 2014, Brian Simmonds chair for Leicester Black History Consortium produced a separate brochure of events during October and November (Season) funded by the Consortium.

130

DATE	NATIONAL AND INTERNATIONAL EVENTS	LEICESTER EVENTS
2015		Black History Month's theme in 2015 acknowledged the contribution of jazz icon Billie Holiday, in what was the centenary year of her birth.
		Serendipity launches the programme with Strange Fruit, featuring Carol Leeming, Mellow Baku Ili Sanchea, Lydia Unsudimi and Dee Joseph.
2016	In 2016 Dr Kehinde Andrews, Associate Professor of Sociology founded the first UK undergraduate degree in Black Studies at Birmingham City University. Black studies is an interdisciplinary subject that focuses attention on the experiences, perspectives and contributions of people from the African diaspora.	Serendipity launched Lost Legends project funded by Heritage Lottery Fund and supported by Leicester City Council to celebrate the thirtieth Anniversary of BHM in UK and Leicester in 2017.
		Black History Month (launched by Soweto Kinch and his new album 'Nonagram') recognised the life and work of South African Social Rights activist Desmond Tutu on the occasion of his Eighty Fifth Birthday. It also marked 40 years since the seminal publication The Arts Britain Ignores by Naseem Kahn.
2017		2017 celebrates the thirtieth Anniversary of Black History Month an exhibition at Newarke Houses and Gardens Museum through the duration of October as part of Serendipity's Lost Legends project alongside a website, film and dedicated publication Lost Legends: 30 Years 30 Voices.

Cyrille Regis *(1980)* Photographer Laurie Rampling.

REFERENCES

Adams, T. and Hall, S. (2007) 'Cultural hallmark', *The Observer*, 23 September, p.1

Andrews, K. (2017) 'It's a dangerous fiction that one exam will decolonize Oxford's history degrees',
The Guardian, 30 May, p.1

Bogues, A. (2003) Black Heretics, Black Prophets: Radical Political Intellectuals

Browder, A. T. (1992) *Nile Vally Contobutions to Civilization: Exploring the Myths*, Vol. 1. Institute of Karmic
Guidance.

Clarke, J. H. (1967) in Asante, K. M. (1987) *The Afrocentric Idea.* Temple University Press.

Dabydeen, D. Gilmore, J. and Jones, C. (2007) The Oxford companion to Black British history. Oxford University Press.

Drake, Wizkid, Skepta (2015) *Ojuelegba* [MP3]. Soundcity.

Dunlap, L. L. (2004) *What All Children Need: Theory and Application.* University Press of America.

Garrison, L. (2006) 'Black Cultural Archive', *The Voice*

Hall, S. (1998) 'New Ethnicities', in Procter, j., (eds.) *Writing Black Britain 1948-1998:
An Interdisciplinary Anthology.* Manchester University press, p. 271

Hilliard III, A. G. (1988), Introduction. Stolen Legacy: *Greek Philosophy is Stolen Egyptian Philosophy*,
by James, G. G. M. Reprint edition. San Francisco: Julian Richardson Associates.

Haynes, A. (1983) The State of Black Britain. Hansib publications.

Howe, D. (2010) 'Darcus Howe on Black History', *True Tube*.
Available at https://www.truetube.co.uk/film/darcus-howe-black-history (Accessed 21 June 2017).

Mandela, N. (2003) *Lighting your way to a better future.* 'Address by Nelson Mandela at the launch of Mindset
Network, Johannesburg', *Mandela Foundation*, 16 July. Available at http://www.mandela.gov.za/mandela_
speeches/2003/030716_mindset.htm (Accessed: 21 June 2017)

Mandela, N. *A Selection of Quotes* https://www.nelsonmandela.org/content/page/a-selection-of-nelson-mandela-
quotes (Accessed: 14 August 2017)

Morris, M. (2011) *Black History Month FAQ*s. Available at http://blackhistorymonth.org.uk (Accessed: 10 January 2017)

Obama, B. (2008) 'Barack Obama's New Hampshire Primary Speech', *The New York Times*, 8 January.
Available at http://www.nytimes.com/2008/01/08/us/politics/08text-obama.html (Accessed: 21 June 2017)

Olusoga, D. (2016) 'The reality of being black in today's Britain', *The Guardian*, 20 October, p.1

Rhoden, W. C. (2006) *Forty Million Dollar Slaves: The Rise, Fall and Redemption of the Black Athlete.*
New York: Crown Publishing Group.

Vernon, P. (2013) 'Patrick Vernon Explores how October came to be month in which African Legacy is Celebrated'. *Patrick Vernon Blog*, 24 November. Available at: http://patrickvernon.org.uk/patrick-vernon-explores-how-october-came-to-be-month-in-which-african-legacy-is-celebrated/ (Accessed: 21 June 2017)

Williams, C. (1974) *The Destruction of Black Civilization: Great Issues of A Race From 4500 B.C to 2000 A.D.* Chicago: Third World Press

Woodson, C. G. (2006) *The Mis-Education of the Negro.* The Book Tree. (Original work published 1933).

X, Malcolm. (1964) 'Speech at the Founding Rally of the Organization of Afro-American Unity', in Breitman, G., (eds.) *By Any Means Necessary: Speeches, Interviews, and a Letter by Malcolm X.* New York: Pathfinder Press (1970), pp. 35-67.

Younge, G. (2012) 'Whitewashing Black History Month', *The Guardian*, 1 February, p.1

Kainé Choir perform at Curve, Leicester.

BIOGRAPHIES

ALDERMAN JOSEPH ALLEN

Alderman Joseph Earl Allen has lived in Leicester for over 30 years. In 1980 he became a professional youth and community development officer before becoming an Inner Area Development Officer for the City in 1985. He was the first Black man to be both nominated and elected as a Councillor in Leicester 1987– 1995. A former member of the National Black Caucus 1986 – 1987 and the Convention of Black and Asian Councillors 1995, Joe was initiator for the African Caribbean Working Group in the City Council and its partnership with Black community for the African Caribbean Citizens Forum.

MELLOW BAKU

Mellow Baku, artist and composer of song, spoken word and jazz, performs throughout the UK and internationally. Performing over 500 shows in 15 years in local pubs to concert venues in London and New York, she sees stage, studio and community as spaces to connect, share and explore. She's completed two albums, numerous session recordings and delivered a range of workshops in the public, schools and on hospital wards. Mellow collaborates with musicians in ensembles to orchestras, and also works solo. Her performances range from soulful folk and roots with acoustic guitar to live looping, experimental digital soundscapes and poetry.

PAWLET BROOKES

Pawlet is an accomplished and experienced senior manager and producer who has been at the heart of the development of Black arts centres, from the Nia Centre (Manchester) to the Artistic Director of Peepul Centre (Leicester) and Chief Executive of Rich Mix (London). She has been the Arts Council assessor for a number of Black arts capital projects. Pawlet is the Founder and Executive Artistic Director of Serendipity, a diversity led organisation that initiated and produces LDIF (Let's Dance International Frontiers), an annual festival in Leicester since 2011, and also delivers each year a Black History Month programme for Leicester as well as other projects and publications.

PAMELA CAMPBELL-MORRIS

Pamela Campbell-Morris was born in Gloucester, England and raised in Jamaica and moved to Leicester in 1977. Pamela has worked as a nurse and receptionist and a project manager for the Ajani Women and Girls Centre before becoming the Chief Executive of the Akwaaba Ayeh Mental Health Project. In 2015 she began working at the Senior Citizens West Indian Project and the Ageing Together Project, and at the centre for BME Health. Active in carnival, she was crowned queen twice in 1986 and 1989, and is active in the community running the carnival troupe Bumpa Crew and a weekly community group at the African Caribbean Centre.

BIOGRAPHIES

PAULO CARNOTH

Paulo Carnoth moved to Leicester in 2002, establishing Afro-Kubanza, a scheme of workshops that allows him to share his passion for drumming and jewellery making, running music and arts workshops with diverse cultural groups, schools, colleges, community centres and organisations in the East Midlands. Paulo completed a degree course in Youth and Community Development and in his work seeks to provide a creative atmosphere and space as well as an opportunity to discover hidden talents and a forum to celebrate diversity and the rich culture of Africa.

GEORGE COLE

Councillor George Cole has represented the Western ward of Leicester as a Labour Party member since 2011. A former member of Operation Black Vote's Parliamentary Shadowing Scheme, he cites a strong presence in the fight for increased political literacy in the African Caribbean community in Leicester, and participation in the scheme as the inspiration that led him to stand for election. Councillor Cole is also co-founder of the Clarion Group, a Leicester based organisation, which aims to address the absence of African Caribbeans from local politics.

136

DERRICK 'MR MOTIVATOR' EVANS

Derrick Errol Evans, better known as 'Mr. Motivator' is a Jamaican-born British exercise instructor, who rose to fame in the early 1990s through appearances on the UK breakfast television show GMTV, where he became famous for his bright colourful spandex outfits. In addition to his work for television, he has released a number of fitness and workout videos, books, and with his family runs H'Evans Scent, an ecotourism resort, and PaintSplat, Jamaica's first paintball operation. 'Mr Motivator' currently lives in Jamaica and travels all over the world coaching individuals to try and make the world a healthier place.

DOROTHY FRANCIS MBE

Dorothy is the Chief Executive of the Co-operative and Social Enterprise Agency (CASE). She is an award winning business practitioner who, over the course of 33 years in the social business field, has established more than 200 enterprises. In particular Dorothy is committed to promoting business to women, especially women of colour and from newly arrived communities.

BIOGRAPHIES

TONY GRAVES

Tony is Associate Professor for the Arts and Festivals Management, BA undergraduate degree at De Montfort University. He has a background in the arts both as a performer and administrator. A former classical pianist, he is a graduate of the Royal College of Music, and was previously the Chief Executive of The Drum Arts Centre, Birmingham and a producer at Nottingham Playhouse. He is Director of the university's annual Cultural eXchanges festival, and has developed this into a major event over the past 15 years.

CHEDDI GORE

Cheddi Gore is East Midlands Regional Manager for Sported, one of the leading sports development charities in the UK, supporting over 3,000 amazing community clubs and groups that use the power of sport to transform the lives of disadvantaged young people. Cheddi's role is to support Sported members and mentors based in Derbyshire, Nottinghamshire, Northamptonshire, Lincolnshire and Leicestershire and Rutland.

138

PHILIP HERBERT

Philip Herbert studied Music Education at University of Winchester and later at Andrews University, Michigan, USA, with diplomas from the Royal Academy and Royal College of Music. Philip has taught music at all educational levels as well as making music through composing and performing, working with young people and collaborating with some of Britain's finest musicians. He has also been involved in musical projects that have been broadcast on BBC Radio 2, 3 and 4 as well as BBC TV. His work includes 'Elegy – in memoriam for Stephen Lawrence', 'Courante' a suite for solo steel pan and strings, and 'Silent Aria' for oboe and piano.

DONNA JACKMAN

Donna Jackman was born on the Caribbean island of Nevis and moved to Leicester aged 11, and has lived and worked in the Highfields area of the city for most of her life. One of the founder members of Ajani Women's and Girls Centre, an initiative to empower, represent and engage African heritage women, girls and their families, she also was Chair of Leicester African Caribbean Arts Forum (LACAF).

139

BIOGRAPHIES

LOUISE KATEREGA

Louise Katerega is a dancer and choreographer especially acknowledged for her national and international development work for and with disabled people. Louise trained at London Contemporary Dance School, Coventry University and holds a degree in Film and Literature from the University of Warwick. She currently serves as a board member for several local and national dance organisations.

DUNCAN LAWRENCE

The younger of two sons born to Jamaican parents (Lloyd Lawrence, Serviceman and Elisa Lawrence, Community Midwife), Duncan was born in England but grew up mostly in South Wales. He left to study IT, Media and Society at Portsmouth University where he realised a passion for music. He took up the saxophone and became a DJ for the University and worked in student radio. His media skills play an important part in his current career as a professional voice-over artist for a business he established in 2016 (Sound Liaison Limited).

CAROL LEEMING

Carol Leeming is a Fellow of the Royal Society for the Arts (RSA) and recognised polymath; from artist, poet, and playwright to singer, songwriter and presenter. Carol's songs have featured on the sound tracks for *Trainspotting* and *Angie*. Carol was shortlisted for the *Imison Tinniswood Award* for her Radio Drama Reality Check broadcast on BBC Radio 4. Other works include choreopoems, *The Loneliness of the Long Distance Diva* (Curve, 2012), *Love the Life you Live...Live the Life You Love* (2014). Carol's poetry has been published in Black British Poets (Bloodaxe and Newcastle University) and her own debut collection *Declamations* of Cool Eye (2016).

MICHAEL LEWIS

Michael Lewis is Head of Libraries at Shropshire Council. Prior to that he was the senior library manager and senior community librarian for Leicester City Council. During Michael's time working with libraries, he has worked to establish access to African Caribbean collections, and raise the profile of Black History Month within library services.

BIOGRAPHIES

IRIS LIGHTFOOTE

Iris Lightfoote has a BA in Social Sciences and an MA in Criminology from the University of Leicester, a Cropwood Fellow at Cambridge University and has an Honorary Doctorate from Loughborough University. After working at Nottingham and Leicester City Councils, Iris joined The Race Equality Centre as a criminal justice officer, becoming Chief Executive in 2001. TREC is a charity established to champion racial justice through a number of service provisions and as Chief Executive Iris has brought about significant development in the strategic importance and functioning of The Race Equality Centre, enabling the organisation to be a key participant in local policy debates.

TARA LOPEZ

Whilst studying dance at De Montfort University, Tara's passion for culture and education began whilst volunteering for Serendipity and arts and cultural based events and organisations in Leicester. Since then Tara has worked in a variety of roles both in and out of the arts world. She has undertaken research for dance projects such as British Dance and the African Diaspora (BDAD), working alongside choreographer Henri Oguike as a dancer for Let's Dance International Festival (LDIF), managing PR and marketing for national sporting bodies and events, and since 2016 has been working as Tour Manager for the East Midlands Caribbean Carnival Arts Network (EMCCAN).

MADU MESSENGER

Madu Messenger is a vocalist/lyricist and works with the internationally known UK dub reggae group *Vibronics*. As a post-graduate of De Monfort University, with a focus on media and immigration and its relationship with history, he has been able to capture moments of historical struggles faced by Black communities in the lyrics found in *Vibronics meets Brain Damage* album. His other work *Empire Soldiers* is a historical conceptual work that tells the stories of soldiers of colour who fought during WW1. Madu also works as a graphic designer and digital artist; his work has featured on albums and billboards.

ELVY MORTON

Elvy Morton was born in Nevis and came to England and worked as a nurse in Birmingham, moving to Leicester after she married. She continued to work in Leicester before training and becoming a professional chef at Southfields College, now Leicester College. Elvy studied further at Wyggeston College, teaching adults and children there and at Moat Community College. In 1984, the hundred and fiftieth anniversary of the abolition of the slave trade in the British Caribbean islands, Elvy set up Leicester Caribbean Carnival and was chairperson for 18 years, and is still involved, she also volunteers at the African Caribbean Centre.

BIOGRAPHIES

FLORENCE CHANAKIRA-NYAHWA

Florence Nyahwa came to Leicester and set up the African international organisation that works for better education across cultures and people of difference that was named the S M Nyahwa Foundation (SMNF). In partnership with Christians Aware, SMNF has a joint project called "Listen to Africa" (L2A), and it organises lectures, exhibitions, workshops and visits to Africa and the Caribbean islands. L2A hosts an in-house annual seminar on topical issues relating to African heritage communities based here in the UK or overseas.

SUZANNE OVERTON-EDWARDS

Suzanne grew up in London, attending King's College, University of London to study physiology and was awarded a PGCE from the Institute of Education. In her early career, she taught biology and chemistry, and was later appointed to Haringey's Adult Education Service to establish numeracy courses. She was appointed as the Lifelong Learning Co-ordinator at the College of North East London, before becoming Vice Principal of City of Westminster College, and Principal of Gateway College, Leicester. She is a member of Leicester Children's Trust Board, a governor at Hamilton Community College, a board member of De Montfort University and a trustee of Leicester Arts Centre.

144

SHAKHA PALMER

Shakha Palmer is the co-founder of Active Learning and Leicester Community Radio. Active Learning develop projects that seek to have a positive impact on the local and wider community, championing equality and diversity and challenging policies that change or devalue the impact on vulnerable communities. A major success is the 'Think Community' Radio Show on Leicester Community Radio and in 2016 'Think Community' held a Police and Crime Commissioner Election campaign (PCC) live on air. The organisations act as a beneficial support network through advocacy, signposting and service users to useful resources and personal administration services.

VICTOR RICHARDS

The London-born Leicester-bred son of Barbadians, Windrush actor, writer, poet and storyteller. Victor has written and performed three one man plays, *Streets Paved with Gold, Return to the Caribbean* and *Children of the First Generation*. He has also produced a unique poetry production entitled *I Spy Through the World's Eye* to delighted audiences in the UK and internationally as far as Japan. His book *Poetry Trilogy* was published in 2008, the spoken word with reggae music album *Illusion – Streets Paved with Gold* was released in 2015. He is preparing special events on tour for the seventieth Windrush anniversary 2018.

145

BIOGRAPHIES

BRAIN SIMMONDS

Brain Simmonds is the Chairperson for Leicester Black History Consortium (LBHC), which is a community organisation that promotes and delivers Black history events throughout the year culminating in a community based Black History Season in October and November. He also works as a youth advocate for the Leicester City Council and was previously Director of Cherub Community Ventures.

GREGORY SMITH

Gregory Smith has over 30 years' experience as musician, vocalist and songwriter. Gregory is the Director of Kainé Management, which he co-founded with Maxine Chambers, organising and delivering Gospel arts programming, and recruiting and training workers to deliver opportunities.

146

JULIE D. SMITH

Julie is Serendipity's Project Manager, having over 20 years' experience of working in the public, private and voluntary sectors. She has a background in the arts both as a performer and administrator. A former De Montfort University student, Julie graduated with a BA (Hons) in Performing Arts (Dance). Julie has worked with a number of cultural organisations within the East Midlands region including Phoenix Arts Centre, Kaine Management Group, Peepul Centre, the Centre Gallery, Leicester Comedy Festival, Locostandu Dance Company, LeicestHERday, Foot in Hand Dance Company, Spark Children's Festival, Leicester Haymarket Theatre and Midlands Arts Marketing.

DIANNE VAN-DER-WESTHUIZEN

Dianne was born in Johannasburg, South Africa and moved to Leicester in 1968 and has lived in Highfields ever since. Establishing herself as part of the community she has worked in a variety of roles, and is currently a ward clerk at Leicester Royal Infirmary.

BIOGRAPHIES

BOSTON 'THE ORATOR' WILLIAMS

The Orator is a Poet. His parents are from Montserrat and Jamaica, and his passion is the pursuit of a life in the art of storytelling. From delivering workshops in modern Black leadership at the University of Gambia to demonstrating against antifascism across the UK, The Orator is as politically active as well as he is artistically active. Early 2017 sees the release of *Vernacular, The Poetry Album*. Late 2017 sees the release of *Vernacular, The Orator's debut Poetry Collection*. Whether it's through print, record or live everybody is encouraged to get involved with this young man's journey.

QUINCY

Quincy is regarded as one of the best of a new wave of comics to come out of the UK. Quincy received recognition by doing warm-ups for the hit TV show Blouse and Skirts on BBC One and becoming a finalist in Gagging For It in 2000, the Leicester Mercury new act of the year 2001 and BBC New talent showcase 2002. Quincy turned a full time Comedian in 2005 and went on to win the best break-through act at the Black Entertainment Comedy Awards and headlining at clubs around the UK before starting his own club in 2007.

FREEDOM TARIQ ZAMPALADUS

Freedom is a community facilitator, entrepreneur, author, equestrian specialist and motivational speaker. He is passionate about improving his community, he has a vast range of youth and community involvement both overseas and locally and has pioneered many of those projects, providing services and learning experiences for clients such as Leicester City Council, mainstream education and other service providers such as Connexions. Freedom also works with Black Poppy Rose to honour African, African Caribbean and Pacific Island people who contributed to the war effort.

66 Black history is not a subgenre of history. Nor does it stand apart from other histories. It makes no more or less sense than American history, Jewish history or Tudor history. Nor is it any more or less diverse — black historians don't agree on everything just because they're black. Partial, interconnected, necessary, it is simply the world's history told either about or through the prism of a particular group of people. **99**

Gary Younge (2012)

150